AUTISM AND THE POWER OF MUSIC

A New Approach to Help Your Child Connect and Communicate

YASMINE WHITE

WITH SONIA BELASCO

Endorsements

"This book is an eye-opening experience. It offers parents new insights and tools to learn with and from their child and adult."

— Lori Ireland
Chair of the Board of Directors, Autism Society of America

"This remarkable book offers a compelling therapeutic approach that harnesses music as a way to promote communication and social skills. Backed by science, the VOICSS® model will be useful for teachers, caregivers, and clinicians who seek to help people on the autism spectrum reach their full potential. Written in a way that is both compassionate and practical, this book is highly recommended!"

— Geraldine Dawson, PhD
William Cleland Distinguished Professor of Psychiatry
Director, Duke Center for Autism and Brain Development
Duke University

"In the book *Autism and The Power of Music*, Yasmine White shares her decades of experience as a Music Therapist with practical and creative strategies to promote active engagement and trusting relationships with autistic people of all ages. As a clinician, researcher and performing musician, I found her innovative, evidence-based VOICSS® model to resonate beautifully with our Uniquely Human philosophy and SCERTS educational model. Yasmine's emphasis on social communication, emotional regulation, and supportive relationships embodies the most effective, cutting-edge approaches for supporting autistic individuals. *Autism and The Power of Music* is a much-needed resource for parents to connect with their children through music and will also be embraced by educators and clinicians who wish to infuse joyful learning experiences in their work."

— Barry M. Prizant, CCC-SLP
Brown University
Author, Uniquely Human: A Different Way of Seeing Autism *and* The SCERTS Model *manuals*

Endorsements

"*Autism and the Power of Music* will show you how something as simple as tapping on an improvised drum can completely change how you connect and communicate with your child on the autism spectrum. This book offers a multitude of ways to apply music in everyday situations. A rhyme, a simple melody, or a basic rhythm can open the door for both parent and child to grow and connect in new ways. It can be a game changer, especially when more traditional approaches have not been successful. This book is a wonderful starting point for putting the VOICSS® model to work in your home."

> — Jonathan Chase
> *Author, Autism/Autistic Advocate*

"*Autism and the Power of Music* is a unique way and concept of building generalization skills in individuals with autism and other developmental disabilities. I applaud the efforts of the authors in exploring the science behind their strategies and giving practitioners a solid method to implement. I would highly recommend this book to families, teachers, speech and language therapists, and all those who work with people with autism and/or other developmental disabilities."

> — James Ball, Ed.D., BCBA-D
> *President/CEO, JB Autism Consulting*
> *Honorary Board Member, National Board of Directors,*
> *Autism Society*
> *Past Two Time/Interagency Autism Coordinating Committee/*
> *Community Member*

AUTISM AND THE POWER OF MUSIC
A New Approach to Help Your Child Help Themselves

All marketing and publishing rights guaranteed to and reserved by:

FUTURE HORIZONS INC.

(800) 489-0727
(817) 277-0727
(817) 277-2270 (fax)
E-mail: info@fhautism.com
www.fhautism.com

ISBN: 9781949177725

Dedication

To little Katie whose light shined as
long as she was given to shine.

Contents

Author's Note

Languaging in the world of autism is in transition. I have chosen to use "person-first" language that identifies the individual as a person first. In other words, I use the phrase "person with autism" or "person who has autism" rather than "autistic person" or "autistic child." I am aware that there are many individuals on the spectrum who want to be identified as "autistic," making autism that person's defining quality, and by choosing person-first languaging, I am not arguing that this is preferable. As we move through this transition, please know that I respect and am listening to all voices.

Following the lead of Barry Prizant in his book *Uniquely Human*, I use the term "nonspeaking" for individuals who do not communicate by speaking. While the term "nonverbal" is often used to describe these individuals, they are verbal, since they often communicate using sign language or adaptive devices.

Acknowledgments

I was told many years ago that when you create something, it should come through you and not from you. This book, after many years, found its way through me, and I am so happy to be able to offer it to parents and anyone who can benefit from it. It is a culmination of the support and expertise of many people along the way: colleagues, families, individuals on the spectrum, individuals who are otherwise neurodivergent, music therapists throughout the years who have been a part of the evolution of the VOICSS® model, and of course, my family.

Thanks to:

First and foremost, the children, teens, and adults—and their families—who have shared in the joy of our program model over the years. Thank you for your trust and for sharing yourselves and your family members.

My collaborator, Sonia Belasco, for her ability to shape the content while keeping the intention of the words and project true to its original feel and purpose. An author in her own right, she very gracefully helped bring the book to its clear intention.

My husband, Jim White, who has always offered me "The Big Space" where I am reminded that possibilities are where we live. I am grateful for his never-ending patience and support for my abilities and sass.

My sons, Spencer and Nick, who are now making their own place in the world with drive, compassion, and creative intelligence. They participated in this journey while they were growing up and have now become part of my team of support and advisors.

My parents, who taught me love and resilience.

My grandmother, whose strength, love, and support have guided me.

My sister, Audrey, whose love and support is a phone call away in the good and bad times.

Andy, who became a friend of the family and opened up a new perspective for me.

All the VOICSS® music therapists who have helped this model evolve and grow through the years. They are always an inspiration for their compassion, skills, creativity, and dedication to our clients.

Hailey Kaiter, MT-BC VOICSS® music therapist, for her help in compiling articles and resources and for always being willing and interested to jump into a new learning moment enthusiastically.

Wendi Su, for her kind and smart help wherever needed throughout this process.

Acknowledgments

Kristie Matocha, for her dedication to our organization, her special perspective as a parent, and for her wonderful personal story and quote at the beginning of this book.

John Mitterling, for his sound advice and kind support.

Rebecca Stern, for sharing her son with us through the years and for her advice, friendship, and her quote in this book.

Carey Jones, my copy editor, for her friendly nature and her time and skill.

The Voices Together past and present Board of Directors for their advice, expertise, support, and enthusiasm. A special thank you to Dr. Phillip Buchanan and Caterri Woodrum for their endless hours generously given to our organization and for believing in me and believing in the journey.

The Voices Together Advisory Council, for their time, expertise and special friendships.

Florence Peacock, for so deeply understanding the importance of our vision and being a true supporter and friend from the beginning.

Lori and Gregg Ireland, for their support and friendship throughout the years and for sharing Vinnie with us.

Geraldine Dawson, PhD, for her friendship, advice, and advocacy for the VOICSS® program model. Her support and collaboration opened doors for us.

Tom Nechyba, PhD, for his support and for giving Voices Together the opportunity for a research partnership with Duke University.

Lorrie Schmidt, PhD, for her friendship and endless collaborative work and for bringing important and accurate evaluation to our model.

Terri Shelton, PhD, for her support and advice and for writing the foreword for this book.

JoAnn and Larry Currie, for their support and for sharing their memory of Brenna with us.

Douglas Zinn, Dorian Burton, and The William R. Kenan, Jr. Charitable Trust, who have helped bring this special model of music therapy into the lives of so many.

I want to thank all of the donors and foundations who have supported us, lifted us in times of struggle, and sustained our vision throughout the years.

North Carolina legislators, school board members, and administrators who took the time to observe and support the program, and the teachers who became partners.

Jonathan Chase, for his expertise, his music, his time, and his genuine friendship.

Acknowledgments

Barry Prizant and John Donvan, for their advice, and Jim Ball, for his amazing support in helping this book become published.

Rose Heredia-Bechtel, Teresa Corey, and the team at Future Horizons for giving me this opportunity.

In memory of Perry Colwell, for being my first mentor and for becoming a true friend.

Anders Bundgaard, for the book cover design.

Foreword

Music is the universal language ... or so said Henry Wadsworth Longfellow over 200 years ago. And with this guide, Yasmine White, CEO and Founder of Voices Together, puts that universality and the power of music in the hands of parents and families of children with autism. Like any parents, parents whose children have been diagnosed as being on the spectrum want the best for their children: to be loved and accepted, and to thrive and live a self-determined life. But we also know that there are particular challenges with autism. Many have difficulties with social interactions, with communicating with others and in understanding others' communications, with managing verbal, auditory, tactile stimuli. And for some, these challenges cause understandable frustration that results in behavioral outbursts, and those outbursts can further detract from the loving and supportive connections from family and friends that we as humans need. So to have a way, a tool, that could not only disrupt these challenges but could propel your precious child toward success is such a gift.

And that is just what this book does. There are many available interventions that enhance the successful outcomes of children with autism, including applied behavior analysis, social skills training, occupational therapy, physical therapy, sensory integration therapy, and the use of assistive technology, but the VOICSS® model is truly unique. First, it is non-directive, and that very characteristic enhances its efficacy. As someone who previously worked in early intervention, I have seen that even the most rigorous, evidence-based strategies, while successful, can engender some pushback. And it is one thing to manage those challenging behaviors in a one-hour therapy session once a week, but it is another as a parent to be put in that situation day in and day out. Secondly, the approach is based on music. What parent hasn't had the chance to share a song with their child? And it is empowering to learn how to harness that enjoyable activity and really tailor it to one's child in an activity that is so normative. Third, while other interventions also provide the child with new skills, and some provide parents new tools, the approach in this book specifically enhances the relationship itself, leveraging that one-of-a-kind connection... not as another one of the child's therapists but in that unique role as parent, grandparent, or those special individuals that are "chosen" family.

I have seen the "magic" that happens. Engagement, smiles, increased eye contact, sustained attention that enhance the child's ability to learn from the day-to-day events. It also can become a valuable adjunct to other therapies that the child may be receiving. To have an interaction that is affirming, fun, and successful, that builds on the child's strengths and preferences and enhances their interest in engaging and ability to sustain that engagement increases the chance that all other encounters, whether with their friends, their families, or with therapists and teachers, will be successful.

Anthony Storr, in his book *Music and the Mind*, stresses that in all societies, a primary function of music is collective and communal, to bring and bind people together. Through this book, families will find a new and innovative approach that will bring and bind them together with their child that will help them to find their own power, their own purpose, and their own voice.

— Terri L. Shelton, Ph.D.

Interim Provost and Vice Chancellor for Research and Engagement

Carol Jenkins Mattocks Distinguished Professor

The University of North Carolina at Greensboro

Introduction

My son has autism and did not talk until he was four years old. We didn't have a real diagnosis until years later, but I kept looking for answers. The one constant during that time was that I sang to him. I sang all the time, every day, everywhere. I sang to move us from doing one thing to another or sang when we were feeling a certain way. It always helped. Somehow, we just connected when we were singing. He would sing with me even though he couldn't talk.

— Kristie Matocha

(personal testament to author, February 13, 2019)

We all want to connect. Connection grows when you and your child feel safe. Your child wants to feel safe. They want to be able to speak without worrying about being judged, ridiculed, or shut down. Your child wants to feel success. Everyone does. They want to connect with others. They want to have purpose. They want to be liked.

The tools and strategies in this book will help you understand your child, help you connect with your child in new ways, and help your child gain tools to help themselves. They offer a way to provide a safe place for your child to begin to understand themselves, know themselves, and express themselves. The approach I set out in this book is called "the 50/50 Approach"—a way to meet your child with autism halfway. This book assumes that we can both learn from each other.

To do this, we need to meet halfway and offer tools, support, and safety to build a common ground where we can begin the process of learning about each other. When we decide that we are going to meet someone halfway, we are not on a mission to change or fix them, but rather, we are trying to work together on understanding and supporting the person we love. Understanding and acknowledging your child's unique strengths and searching for the reasons behind their behavior can open new channels of communication and growth. This approach offers tools to help parents recognize their child's unique perspective and create opportunities to meet them halfway. It helps parents find solutions and guide their child through hard moments. It also helps them look for the emotions that are fueling negative behaviors and are barriers to connection. Parent and child can find these emotions together, work to break down barriers, and gain the ability together to navigate difficult situations.

I am a music therapist, and in my experience, music is one of the most powerful tools to connect us all in ways that might otherwise be difficult. The techniques in this book are based on a specialized music therapy model I developed that focuses on social communication and emotional regulation using the 50/50 approach. Ideas on how to use music to support change and offer ways to engage and connect are seamlessly woven through the book. Music can unlock language, bring us together socially, and help us express our deepest emotions. It can help us communicate when language is hard, feel when feelings are hard, and help us connect when being with others is hard. Music structures the body and mind and calms and focuses the nervous system. Music motivates us as a pleasurable experience. It is an engagement tool, an attention-getter, and an easy, non-threatening, and enjoyable way to experience shared time with someone else.

These techniques are based on what has been called a "humanistic" approach. It contrasts with many other approaches to autism, which are based on identifying behaviors and trying to change them to ones more "appropriate" for our society.

But I believe that behavior is a symptom, and behaviors tell us a story. Ultimately, our behaviors tell a story that stems from our need to express something vital about our experience that we cannot find the words for. In other words, if a child is hitting, we do want them to stop this behavior—but it's the "why" they are hitting that is the key to their change.

Parents who have a child on the spectrum often are scrambling to make sense of what tools and systems will work with their child. This book offers some strategies to help. The tools do not require any special skills. This book offers a way to ease the path for each parent to understand, guide, and connect with their child, and for each child coming into the world with autism, to help them find their own power, their own purpose, and their own voice.

When you see a box like this, it is a "tool" section. These sections will give you more hands-on practical ways to try some of these motivating and effective tools and techniques.

CHAPTER 1
The 50/50 Approach

When we decide that we are going to meet someone half-way, we establish that we are not on a mission to change or fix them, but rather to mutually understand and support the person we love.

I'll meet you where you are, not where I want you to be. I will listen to you, watch you, and accept you. I will try and understand and accept the "why" of your actions. I will ask you. I know you have your own way of seeing things. I will tell you that you can, I know that you are able, and I accept that you will always bring parts of you to the moment. It's a compromise: I will give you choices and some ideas, things that will help you understand what to do. One at a time. Then we will work together towards change.

We all take in the world in a unique way, and we all have something unique to say about our experience on this earth. Direct interaction with our day-to-day world drives our actions and reactions. It is a give-and-take, a back-and-forth, or, in musical terms, a "call and response." If the sun is out, we squint; if it's rainy, we tend to hibernate; and if an environment feels threatening to us, we will respond differently than if a situation or person is open and welcoming.

In the early 1990s, I was a music therapist practicing in Los Angeles. At that time, there were few individuals with autism who had published material from their perspective or who were able to express their perspective. It seemed like the only approach that was being practiced and talked about was helping children with autism stop their "autistic" behaviors. Parents were searching for answers that were hard to find. When you don't understand the challenges, all you have to go on are the behaviors.

Often, I would travel to my clients, most of whom were families who lived in wealthy neighborhoods in Southern California and could afford many interventions for their children. One of my first clients was a family living in the Pacific Palisades. The parents had two sons, ages six and eight, both of whom were on the spectrum. I had been advised by their parents to keep the boys as structured and as busy as possible so they wouldn't have enough time to "stim," a term that stood for self-stimulation—repeated movements, words, or sounds—common to many people with autism. The common thought at the time was that if the children were "stimming," they were not paying attention to the things that they should be paying attention to. The goal was to alter that particular behavior. In other words, train the child through behavioral drilling to stop the stimming, and by doing so, help the child pay attention and learn behaviors that would lead to being "normal."

One day I arrived at 3 PM with my music therapy "bag of tricks" and walked into the living room. The last therapist had just left 10 minutes before, and here I was, ready to begin. The boys had been occupied with different interventionists since the morning. They saw me and burst out crying. I had never had that happen! Kids usually loved when I showed up with all my instruments and songs. But really, could I blame them? They hadn't been allowed any breaks. Although the activities we were going to do might have been engaging, they were still structured and goal-oriented and were meant to expand their language abilities and social connection. They were being asked to go outside their comfort zone, which could be exhausting. Every human being, especially a small child, needs downtime from structured activities.

Although the parents—and the professionals they'd hired—were trying to support the children by intervening at a young age with every support available, they weren't beginning from where these children were. The boys had unique needs, and although their parents were making every effort to understand those needs, the techniques they were given did not allow them to meet their children halfway.

When we decide that we are going to meet someone halfway, we establish that we are not on a mission to change or fix them, but rather to mutually understand and support the person we love. We want to not only understand them and their perspective as best as we can, but also to make sure we continue to listen and watch as they change. We want to explain the hard steps to change and give them choices that will help engage them in their own growth, while at the same time keeping in mind that compromise is always a part of change and growth.

As a therapist, I see my relationship with each client as a partnership. This is one way I am able to help. I enjoy the uniqueness of every person I work with. I enjoy the process of trying to understand their story. I know that if they can't tell me what they need or want, it is important to give them the tools to communicate and interact. It is vital that they feel they have a voice and that someone is listening.

A 50/50 Approach

It's 50/50 when you assume your child can find a way to tell you what they need, want, and feel, with your help if necessary. It is a problem-solving mission that includes questions, structure, and practicing communication and steps to understand each other.

I have developed a model that acknowledges that each person's experience and way of seeing the world is unique to them and takes each person's needs into account. It is called VOICSS®, which stands for Vocal Interactive Communication and Social Strategies. VOICSS® focuses on creating a fun, safe environment that improves emotional regulation, social, and communication skills and helps individuals who have difficulty connecting with others feel successful. It uses a group structure and employs techniques from music therapy, and it is designed to be accessible to everyone. There is no developmental or particular skill level needed. Both verbal and nonspeaking children can participate fully. The program works with all ages, from pre-K to adults.

This book is designed to help you implement the principles of the VOICSS® model with your child in simple, effective ways. VOICSS® uses a non-directive approach when working with others, which, in my experience, has proven more preferable than directing a child to behave a certain way. When children make change themselves, it not only is more empowering for them, but the results will last longer. Your child can create positive change in themself with some guided help. For a younger child, this may seem farfetched; however, this approach is transformational when we take small but significant steps that change the way we interact with our children. When a child is empowered to be a part of their own change, they will gain tools to manage their lives as they grow and become more independent.

VOICSS® group sessions build routine and predictability and elicit guided responses. Children feel comfortable almost immediately and gain success quickly. Although the VOICSS® program is facilitated by board-certified music therapists, parents can implement some of these techniques with their children and achieve remarkable results.

David[1] was a seven-year-old in one of our VOICSS® groups a number of years ago. He was good at language and very capable. David loved everything about dinosaurs and especially enjoyed talking about them. He found the topic comforting

1. *All children's names are pseudonyms.*

and predictable. When we got to our topic song, where there was an opportunity to talk about ourselves within the particular question for that day (such as "What do you like to do at home?" or "What is hard for you at school?"), David would shape his answers around what he wanted to really talk about: dinosaurs.

One day, David answered the question of that day with an answer about dinosaurs. David knew a lot about dinosaurs, and the therapist appreciated and validated the answer as always. Then the therapist took it one step further, asking, "Is there another thing that is fun to do when you are home?" By validating David and building on his safer choice, the therapist was able to develop his ability to step outside his comfort zone in a new way.

Another child, Jack, who was nine years old, felt the need to keep talking for extremely long and extended periods of time without understanding or reading the cues of his peers in his VOICSS® group. The others began making small, impatient noises, and their expressions showed their impatience. The music therapist who was facilitating the group asked Jack to pause for a moment and asked him if he noticed anyone's face in the group. Jack responded, "Oh, what's wrong?" One of his peers responded that Jack was going on too long, and they wanted to give others in the group a chance to talk. Jack said, "I need to make sure you really understand what I am saying." The peer replied, "We already know what you are saying."

The music therapist asked the group members what they thought might help them be able to listen to Jack; they said it would help if he could talk less. Jack heard them, and the music therapist suggested the group come up with a polite signal to help Jack recognize that they understood his story. The group talked about signals they could give him and also came up with the idea of giving each person a time limit to speak. Eventually, they all agreed on signals to use going forward.

The group took the time to learn about why Jack talked for such long periods of time. At the same time, Jack learned that the group couldn't listen for that long a period of time. Everyone worked together to facilitate a better group experience. Jack may never fully be able to read a person or group of people when in a conversation, but he is now aware of why he finds the need to talk things out so fully, and he can tell others why he does what he does. Jack also began gaining tools to adjust his conversational skills in a social situation. This kind of self-awareness, created by experiencing a safe place where someone feels that their perspective is heard and accepted, is the first step to self-advocacy.

So how do you provide a safe place for a child, teen, or adult who is on the spectrum and processes the world in their own way to begin to understand who they are? A place where they can begin to express themselves? Where they can begin to manage their emotions? It has happened in VOICSS® groups, but it can also happen in your own home. You have that power. You have the power to raise their awareness and give them tools to make choices. You have the power to help them help themselves. When they are able to understand their own needs and can convey those needs to others, this will begin their journey to independence.

In the chapters that follow, we will look at how you can use strategies to help your child improve their ability to express and regulate their emotions, communicate, and be more comfortable in social situations. I am excited to share easy, interactive techniques and music-based tools you can use to connect with and empower your child, anywhere and anytime.

CHAPTER 2
Music Is a Place

The music is all they heard. He was wrapped around her tiny frame with his head resting on her shoulder. They were swaying to the music and they were communicating. He had no words and no way to tell her what he felt, thought, or needed, but he had music—and the music connected him to her.

Kevin had sandy brown hair, fair skin, and beautiful blue eyes. At age two, he was beginning to acquire language. But at age three, Kevin stopped talking, and no one knew why until he was diagnosed with autism.

His mother loved music and noticed early on that her son did too. As a way to communicate and remain close to him, she would pick him up. He wrapped his legs around her, and she would hold him tight, put music on, and move around the room to the beat and melody. Sometimes they would rock, sometimes they would sway, and sometimes they would spin. They danced in the living room, the CD player within reach. They danced to folk, classical, jazz, rock, pop, or whatever music or song they enjoyed at that moment. Kevin would put his arms around his mother's neck, his head nestled on her shoulder and an expression of pure bliss on his face. She knew that although she could not speak with her son, during those times when they were dancing, they were completely connected.

Music is a universal language, and Kevin and his mom's shared universe was tied to melody, rhythm, and the music.

Music was their natural connector and defined their time together with no boundaries and no barriers. They couldn't talk about the emotions that they may have been feeling, but they could both feel the emotion of the music, and for that brief period of time, they were in complete sync. From the moment they began to dance, they shared their mutual love of music. Music had become their language and a place where they could communicate.

As Kevin grew, he began to choose the music that they would dance to. The CDs were all kept near the CD player, and Kevin knew which ones he liked. He would reach for one, then point out the song he wanted to his mom. She would put the CD on, then pick him up, and they would move to wherever the rhythm of the song took them. When Kevin had grown to a fairly tall eight-year-old, he still wrapped his long legs around his mom's petite form, and they danced. As they danced, all barriers dissolved, and they sailed together from one musical moment to another.

Music and the Brain

If kept simple, accessible, and purposeful, musical rhythm and melody demand and hold our attention as they set up new patterns in our bodies and minds. Music opens up a new place that has easy patterns and structure. Kevin, like so many others who are neurodivergent, was able to experience how music calms and organizes our neurological system. This is part of what makes music such a powerful tool.

When we listen to or play music, it changes the chemistry of our bodies. For decades, scientists have been studying why and how we play and listen to music. They found that when we listen to music that we are emotionally engaged in, our brain discharges pleasure or reward neurotransmitters into our bodies. Neurotransmitters are chemical messengers that are released by nerve cells throughout the nervous system. One study found that when listening to music that subjects found highly emotional, during peak emotional passages, their brains released dopamine, a "feel-good" chemical. Dopamine plays a key role in the motivational component of reward-motivated behavior in humans. In other words, when dopamine is released, we feel good, and when we feel good, we are naturally motivated and more open to learning and to new things.

Other studies have shown that while the ability to process language can vary widely among people on the spectrum, the receptive and expressive abilities of music-making are often the same for everyone.

Music offers a platform for shared emotional experiences. What I want to do in this book is bring an awareness to what you already might know instinctively about music from your own experience and highlight the different ways that music can act as a tool to communicate, as a way to express emotions, and as a means to connect with others. You can then use your natural instincts, along with enjoyable and effective tools I will provide, to connect to your child and support their growth.

Music Replaces Chaos with Order

Sensitivities to touch, taste, sight, hearing, and the sensory world in general can make it immensely difficult for a child with autism to interact with others. A child with autism may be unable to filter sounds, whether in a classroom, a crowded mall, or a gathering of family and friends. Typical lighting may look like a disco ball, fractured and too bright. A lawn mower starting up may sound like an explosion.

I don't think any of us could be interested in the subtleties of socializing when it feels like we are being attacked by our environment. Our response would naturally be to duck and cover, or find an escape route through distraction. People with the sensitivities of autism cope using all kinds of methods that can seem odd to the outside world. They may become obsessed with twirling a straw and focusing on that straw so that they can ground themselves. They may cover their ears or eyes or make noise to drown out all the other sounds or activity that may be bombarding them. If a child is sensitive in these ways, they may be so focused on what they are experiencing that they have no capacity or motivation to reach out to others. They just want relief and will do whatever they can to get it.

Though your child, like Kevin, may have difficulty processing language and the sensory input from their environment, they can often process music the same way as everyone else. If your child struggles to read social signals, music is easy. It doesn't ask for anything; it just exists in its own space. Music gives you a neutral island to go to in order to connect. For Kevin, music was able to cut through all the other white noise, creating a safe, reliable place that made sense, and it offered routine, structure, and a shared moment with his mother. As Kevin was listening and moving to the music with his mom, they were able to speak the same coherent language. Music not only helped organize Kevin's internal thoughts and feelings, but also helped break down all the external stimuli into something he could understand. Music bonded Kevin with his mother as they shared this special experience and place. With that bond came a type of calm where there was no pressure to do anything other than choose the music and experience social interaction and connection.

Music is a Language

Music has an innate structure that is tied together by rhythm and melody. Lyrics help connect spoken language to all the melodic and rhythmic phrases. This sets up easy patterns for us to grasp. Here's an example: In rap or hip-hop music, the central driving force is the beat. Because of the beat, the lyrics have a place to jump on and take a ride. We hear both the beat and the lyrics, but the beat is like the water, and the lyrics are the boats that sail around and on top of it. They work together. The beat provides the foundational structure for the lyrics and expression. If you watch a hip-hop artist on stage, the beat offers the foundation of the structure, and the lyrics, attitude, and movement all build on that beat, creating order out of chaos as the artist communicates a story.

Neuroscientists have been studying how the parts of the brain that house language and music overlap. Their findings give us reason to believe that singing can help create fertile ground for speaking when speaking on its own may be challenging. For more information on these studies and the ones discussed above, see Resources for Parents, page 199.

If talking is difficult for a child, singing can be a great way to communicate. Similarly to music, language has a structure that incorporates tones and rhythms. Using music to communicate is a natural inclination for all of us. When being with others is hard and a child with autism cannot figure out what he or she is supposed to do or say, a song's rhythm and melody can help them land in language that makes sense for a little while. A song can give a child who doesn't have the words a way to express themselves.

Music is Emotion

Music can also provide children on the spectrum a way to express and regulate their emotions. Music exists in our world as a way to process emotion. Most people have turned to music at one time or another to do just that. For example, stores play music in the background to make you feel good about shopping. A persistent bass beat through speakers at a football game's halftime can create excitement, while quiet string music at the dentist can calm you. Singing along to a driving rock song in the car can help you deal with a frustrating day at work. We use music as a source of comfort or a motivational tool, turning to it when we are sad or grieving or when we want to celebrate.

If your child is on the spectrum, they may have difficulty regulating their emotional states. This does not mean just frustration or anger, but also emotions that may be positive, such as excitement. Our bodies are so fully connected that one area or system is bound to affect another. Emotion is experienced not only in our minds, but also physically in our bodies. Music can be an outlet for frustration and sadness, or a way to blow off steam when a child is feeling overstimulated. When things get difficult for a child on the spectrum in day-to-day life, music can help them connect with their emotions and with you, offering them an enjoyable place to learn and grow.

Music Makes Us Want to Move

Singing and moving are natural for all of us. As children, we are not self-conscious about how we might appear to others. We sing and dance spontaneously and freely. As we grow, we lose that spontaneity. We become more aware of ourselves, our bodies, and social norms, and are less likely to freely sing, move to a beat, or outright dance. We may feel we need permission to do these things—for example, at a nightclub with music where others are dancing, or if someone has told us we are good at singing and dancing, or we've taken music or dance lessons. The rest of us may stay still and silent, even though music makes us want to move. But when they are young, children are not self-conscious, so they get into the music, they move, they dance, and they celebrate.

A young child will process their world through both their body and mind, and they need to move. Music provides a wonderful vehicle to help them understand their world. Feeling rhythm and melody in our bodies grounds us, especially at a young age. It helps us build a natural sense of order with the environment around us; think of children marching to a song or pretending to conduct a symphony. Clapping or tapping our feet helps our bodies know where everything is and how it relates to what we are feeling.

Though a child on the spectrum may be distracted by sensory issues, they still have the same needs to move, climb, jump, and bounce as any other child does. Music can help integrate the whole child. For a child who experiences sensory processing challenges, such as difficulty with proprioceptive input (having difficulty sensing where their body is in space), music activities can help. For example, singing a song about pulling while your child pulls a stretchy band or singing a song about bouncing while your child sits on a bouncy ball can help them ground themself and gain sensory information about their body. Music and the rhythm of a song will also help them attend to the activity longer.

Music-making creates opportunities to increase skills for imitation, joint attention, and social awareness. Songs that include movement (like marching songs) or drumming together either on a toy drum or pots and pans can be helpful tools to connect with your child and build necessary skills. You can incorporate waving a colorful scarf into a children's song. There are wonderful instruments that have motor opportunities attached to them for young children. We will explore a few songs and activities in future chapters.

Creating a Sense of "Together"

Being with others and being part of a group is something that young children learn gradually through natural cues and prompts from their parents, teachers, and peers. Routines such as circle time add structure in the classroom for children.

Developmentally, there are many ways that children can learn to jointly play, build awareness of others, and learn social interaction skills. When children are very young, interacting in a peer group for playtime and/or "make believe" helps them build these tools on their own. They become aware of the other person or people in a group and learn to interact in order to get a mutually good experience.

This is not as easy for a child with autism, who may have difficulty reading nonspeaking cues in a social situation. It is hard to pick up on such undercurrents when so many other things are vying for your attention. It's also difficult to understand social cues if your brain does not give you the signals you need. When a child does not have access to the same intuitive cues that other children seem to and has challenges with communication and/or sensory dysregulation, isolation may feel like a safer social solution. How do we help a child who seeks to isolate themselves feel invited into a sense of togetherness?

In the same way that music can give children with autism an alternative way to communicate or express emotions, it can provide a fun yet structured activity that is socially safe and less demanding than conversation and that can help them feel successful so they will reach out again to be with others. Singing a song with other people brings the "together" into moments that may seem miles apart and fragmented by all kinds of challenges. Music can offer a foundation of synchronicity and mutually shared interest with others. You are listening to the same song, clapping the same rhythm, and singing the same melody. Music is one of those places we can reach out to find those easy, jointly enjoyed moments where we are doing something together and feeling successful. Music is a place that gives a child who has a difficult time knowing when to reach out a way to interact without having to work at how.

CHAPTER 3
Music: A Tool for Connection

My husband and I have known since our son Caleb was a year old that music was the current that powered his spirit. Caleb has autism and spoke until he was nine, but he is now nonspeaking. We have used songs to help with every aspect of life, from the mundane to the profound. Caleb's dad and I mourn the loss of Caleb's speaking voice every single day. Music is the terrain on which we meet.

> — Rebecca Stern
> (personal testament to author,
> February 13, 2019)

We interact with music in our lives in all kinds of ways. We can be passive listeners: sometimes we are not really aware of the music, or it is relegated to the background of whatever we are doing. Sometimes music warms up an atmosphere or supports an activity. We can also develop music as a skill, such as getting better at singing or playing an instrument. This chapter is about using music as a tool with your child to help them learn, grow, and explore themself while connecting with others.

Getting Started

Over the years, parents have often asked me where to start when trying to use music to engage with their child. My answer always begins the same way: What music do you enjoy? What motivates you? What is fun? If you are having fun, your child will have fun, because your enthusiasm is contagious. If you are motivated, then they will be motivated. As you work with your child and they learn, you will learn as well. What songs do I like? What excites us? What makes us want to move? What music does my child seem to enjoy? What captures their attention and takes them to a new place? The best place to begin is to genuinely want to engage with your child and have fun.

Being Present

Engaging with your child also requires you to be completely present in the moment. Being present with another person sounds so easy in theory, but it may not be in practice. We bring all of our thoughts, worries, and planning to each moment, and often we are either thinking about what just happened yesterday or today or about what we want to do in the future. Most people are rarely in the present moment for very long. To be fully present, we have to let go of our ideas of what this time with another person is supposed to look like or what we are supposed to get out of it. We need to watch, listen, share, and open up to whatever may happen while allowing your child to be who they are.

Music should be a pleasurable tool for engagement. It should be a time to connect with your child in a fun and motivating activity. This should not turn into a power struggle or a chore for either of you. The point is to find that moment when you are both enjoying yourselves together, and all you have to do is gently form a "together moment." The only tools you need are recorded music, toy or real instruments, your voice, clapping hands or stomping feet, and an open mind.

"Find the Beat"

Before you engage with your child using music, you will first need to get comfortable with finding the beat yourself. Wherever you are—in the car, out with friends, at home in the kitchen or backyard—if you hear music, pause and allow yourself to really feel the song. Put your hand on your chest and tap out the rhythm along with the song you are hearing. It's there. It's all there, in the beat. It makes us want to tap our feet, bounce our heels, clap our hands, and move our heads. That's the heart of the music. The beat is the engagement tool. It's the tool that can connect you and your child like an invisible thread. So, let's "find the beat!"

Rhythm Talk

When you have a moment on your own, say your name out loud. I know this sounds funny, but finding everyday rhythms that we use all the time in our language is a great way to become aware of and comfortable with how rhythm plays a role in how we speak as well as how we play. Using a rhythm game is an enjoyable way to engage your child and increase language while having fun. So for example, if your name is Catherine, where are the syllables and how do you sound them out? You can break it up into three syllables—"Cath-er-ine"—or say it all in one quick beat: "Catherine." Play with your name. If you're driving and have stopped at a red light, try to tap out a rhythm on your steering wheel, then put your name to that rhythm. Try to get into "play" mode. All of these small steps will bring you closer to that part of you that as a child was so comfortable playing with sounds, singing, and using rhythm. This has nothing to do with skill or musical talent— this is just about having fun. We have rhythm housed inside of us. When you get comfortable saying your name in rhythm, tap it out. For example: "Cath-er-ine," tap, tap, tap. Then, put it in a sentence where you tap out each of the syllables in your name: "My name is Cath-er-ine." Once you get used to hearing the rhythm in words, try it with your child and his/her name. If you get comfortable and used to thinking of rhythm as a part of communication and a way to interact with your child, all sorts of fun ways to engage will open up.

Find Your Voice

Next comes the part where you are in the shower and you al-low yourself to test out your speaking voice morphing into a singing voice. It does not have to be a beautiful voice. It is re-discovering the voice you used to sing with as a child before you knew the difference between a "good voice" and a "bad voice." So, say your name and notice if it sounds like it stays on one note. If you say it, most likely it will. Now try and take each of those syllables in your name and sing them out. There is no right or wrong note. Breathe and sing. You can sing your name or another sentence like "I am taking a shower now." What kind of rhythm does "wash my hair" have? Clap it out: "wash-my-hair." Remember that the purpose is to recall the fun in music play and find an ease with it so you can be free to create these games with your child.

Find the Beat

Once you've found the beat with your own voice, you can start doing it with your child. Find a time during the day when you can build a small routine to play with music-making. Sing or tap out a rhythm on a pot, pan, drum, or other surface. A child with autism may be more interested in the object or the sound they are making with the object than in anyone around them. Notice what they seem to be interested in and whether they look up at a particular sound or rhythm. Watch as your child plays during the day and see if they begin to tap something out and enjoy its sound and feel. Take their lead and try sitting next to them, then tap out the same rhythm on a surface and see if you gain their attention. Then join them and try playing the same beat with them. One way to gain their attention is to stop their tapping motion with your hand for just a few seconds, wait until they look up, say "Wow!" or another sound of praise, then let go of their hand and continue to play together. We will talk more about those "wow" moments in the chapters to follow. Moving from "I am interacting with this sound or object" to "I am interacting with this sound or object *and* my parent" is a powerful moment to build on. You are not asking them to stop interacting with the object; you are asking them to allow you to join for a few moments. This is 50/50, a compromise, a moment of growth and connection for both of you.

Tools You Can Use

Wooden spoons, toy music mallets, or toy drums, pots and pans, your hands—many things around you can be used to make rhythms and music. For younger children, pat-a-cake has a natural beat that helps the child follow your hands, play with you, and coordinate their movements.

Find a song. The music tools and activities below can be used with children of different ages—I recommend going by what you think your child might enjoy. These can also be modified as your child grows. I have included a few thoughts for older children and teens at the end of this chapter (See "Music for the Older Child," page 40). It is important that as your child grows, music that they access is age-appropriate; this can allow for connection with peers.

Put on different kinds of music when you are with your child—vary the place and time. It can be in the evening or before dinner. It can be on a Saturday when you are in the car, or in the afternoon driving home. Turn on music when you are cooking in the kitchen, or put music on when you're doing a puzzle with your child on the floor. Some children like having a "quiet listening corner" in their bedroom, complete with a bean bag, headphones, and music. As far as genre goes, you can try children's songs that you like. Or venture out further to rock, pop, dance songs, or classical music. What resonates with you? Have you noticed your child responding to music before? If so, what have they liked? Have fun with it. Kids can be more sophisticated than we give them credit for. They may like pop songs more than kid songs, or opera instead of pop. You can't know unless you try, so give yourself freedom to explore.

You can talk to your child through music by using your singing voice instead of your talking voice. If you aren't comfortable with singing, try putting your words to a simple rhythm or beat. Putting our words into different, small pieces attached to melody or rhythm can sometimes be the key for a child who has difficulty processing language. If you are having a hard time convincing your child to transition from one activity to another, try singing your request. If thinking up a melody is difficult, use one you already know and put your own practical lyrics to it. For example, try singing, "We are walking to the table now..." to the tune of "The Ants Go Marching."

If your child has sound sensitivity, this may or may not include music listening. It comes down to individual auditory processing and sound tolerance. You may find that if your child is sensitive to music being played, it may be because of the kind of music or the volume, or because too many other things are going on at the same time. Don't assume that if a child responds negatively to one song or one type of music that they are not able to enjoy or tolerate any other music. I have seen some real variations in tolerance that don't follow any patterns. For example, a child may not like recorded music or when you sing but may like to sing themselves. Another child might only like a certain kind of music. Every child is different and has specific preferences. Music is a very personal experience. If your child responds negatively to a musical experience, try problem-solving: ask them questions, and give them choices. For example:

"Should we make it quieter?"
"Do you want headphones?"
"Do you want a new song?"

You may need to give them the words, visuals, or both to help them communicate their choice.

Find a time. Find a moment that you can really just "be" with your child. It needs to be a time in the day when you don't feel pressure to also give your attention to another sibling, your work, or dinner preparation. As a parent myself, I know this is not easy, but all you need to begin is 15 to 20 minutes. Start with twice a week if once a day is too difficult.

Find a quiet place. If a child is having too much difficulty filtering out the many stimulating sounds of a typical day, such as traffic sounds, lights, and the clatter of other family members moving around, find a quiet corner in the house or in their room with comfy chairs and/or a bean bag to sink into. Or, if you prefer to sit on the floor, a small, soft rug is nice. Whatever the setup, you can have a moment together without distraction—just you, your child, and the music. You can use recorded music that your child likes or sing your own. There are picture books for young children that illustrate song lyrics (by Raffi or others)—you can sing together while looking at the pictures. Your child may want to sit next to you or in your lap. Whatever you need to do to take this experience from "you and I" to "us," it's the sharing of this moment that is the foundation of building a sense of "together."

Vary the place or time. A child with autism may latch onto a time, place, or space where you share your musical experience, and they may not be able to experience it anywhere else. Because they struggle so much with trying to find structure in their day-to-day lives, they may feel the need to do the same thing at the same time in the same place when it comes to music. However, this comforting ritual can become a limitation if the routine needs to change for any reason. Trying to build some flexibility within your routine is important.

Move to the beat. Once you've set the musical scene, co-ordinating rhythm and singing begins with feeling the beat in your body. Here are three activities to try with your child.

Talk and Tap Songs

Sit on the floor facing your child. Begin by tapping your fingers on the floor and speaking with each tap:

"The beat, the beat, the beat is on my..." (move your hands to your feet and say "my feet"). Follow this chant with the motion of tapping rhythmically on your feet. Wait to see if your child imitates you with the rhythm and the movement. If not, help them tap. Then say, "the beat, the beat, the beat is on my knees..." as you move your hands to your knees and continue to tap the rhythm. Next, wait and see: if your child initiates a next part on their body to tap, you can imitate them and let them take the lead. If they don't initiate, you can ask, "Where's the beat? Is it on your nose or your head?" (You are modeling tapping those parts of your body to see if they will imitate and join in the game.)

Once you start changing the location of the beat to different parts of your body, they begin to anticipate this change and will look to see what's next. Where is the beat going to land? This creates a natural opportunity for an interaction game.

The objective is to help your child feel the rhythm in their body, coordinate the activity jointly with you, follow directions, and increase their ability to imitate actions. Activities like these will also help them find enjoyment in doing things with you and with others.

Drums Make Me Move

Hand drums work well for music and movement games and activities. These are handheld drums, with or without a mallet, that are easy to play and move to at the same time. You can find them at many online music or children's websites, or at toy stores or music stores. Do an internet search of "hand drums for children" and you'll get many options at different ranges of cost. Remo, a company that specializes in drums of all kinds, offers a set of frame drums in multiple sizes. Companies such as iPlay iLearn Toys also offer child-sized musical instruments. Playing songs that are good to march to or move to with drums in hand can help your child integrate music and their body and connect socially with you. If your child is more interested in spinning with the instrument, you might try stopping the music and spinning together. They will probably look over at you, and when their attention is back on you, you can start the music again and suggest you count together or click instruments in time. Or you can encourage your child to sit down facing you before you start the music again. If the music is a big enough motivator, use it to regain your child's attention on you instead of on the object in hand, building back the sense of togetherness. When your child makes the choice of attending to you rather than an object when playing, give them a big smile and acknowledge their attention with big, positive gestures, words, and affection.

A great instrument and attention-getter is a lollipop drum. The face of the drum is multi-colored like a lollipop. You can order a lollipop drum online or at some music stores (see Resources for Parents, page 199, for more information on where to source musical instruments). This drum is visually engaging, so you can use it as a motivator to get your child's attention in different ways. If you hold the drum up to the right of your face, then they have to look towards you to hit the drum. Giving them a positive response afterward will help them feel successful in putting their attention on you and your face and interacting with you. For a child on the spectrum, looking at someone's eyes can be uncomfortable and/or in some cases painful. Looking in your direction is a good compromise.

If the learning objective is following directions, you can say out loud, "Now, way up high" and lift the drum higher than their height. Lift the drum high enough so the child has to pay attention to where they are aiming, but not so high that it is out of reach. If the objective is to help the child learn to regulate their actions, you can have fun with a start-and-stop game. Put out the drum, and as they hit it, count "3, 2, 1, and..."—put drum facedown on floor or away from the mallet)—"Stop!" Then say "Ready, set, and... go." This game is wonderful for all drums, especially bigger drums that you and your child can play together. If they are able to take the lead, have them take a turn at being the "start-and-stop maker."

Finding Your Sense of Body

Children with autism often struggle with proprioception, the awareness of where their body is in space. Working on this sensory area can help them find balance and grounding in their physical world. Here are a couple of music tools that can help.

Finger Squeeze: This activity can help your child gain a sense of where their bodies are through putting pressure on one part of the body. Use the melody of the ABC song and lightly squeeze each finger as you sing: "Squeeze my fingers, one, two, three, squeeze my fingers, all of me. This is me, this is me, squeeze my fingers, one, two, three."

Stretchy Band Pull: Pushing and pulling an object can be very helpful as well. Take one end of a stretchy band (these can be found online—search for "fidget stretchy band") and give the other end to your child.

Count: "Ready, set, and (wait to see if they say 'go' with you)... go!"

To the tune of Raffi's "Shake my Sillies Out," sing:

"I'm gonna stretch, stretch, stretch the band way out.

Stretch, stretch, stretch the band way out.

Stretch, stretch, stretch the band way out.

Then push it back up to our hands." (At this point, push the band with your hands up against each other so your child can feel the pressure of your hands together.)

Leading the Way

Drums are a great way to take turns with a group of children, whether they are peers or siblings. Everyone can sing a song together, with one child acting as leader to set the rhythm with the drum. Have the child with the drum start to play a rhythm, and then encourage everyone else to sing the song to the rhythm. This offers a child an opportunity to build a sense of pride and self-awareness and sets them up for confidence and self-advocacy as they grow.

Each child is unique; while one activity might capture the attention and joy of one child, it may not appeal to another. It's a trial-and-error kind of adventure and may take a bit of courage at first, but the more you venture in, the more you'll learn and the more comfortable you will feel in the world of music-making.

Music for the Older Child

Having instruments available to a child as they grow, such as a small keyboard, guitar, or percussion instruments, is a great way for them to explore music and their relationship to it. If they are able and show interest, lessons can give them new ways to express themselves and feel successful.

If your child has social and/or communicative challenges, group music therapy can potentially provide a very positive experience and a place to feel socially successful while having fun.

If your child can use a computer or tablet, there are many interesting music games, websites, and software (like *Garage Band*) that allow them to build their own beats, among other fun activities. If your child is willing to do this with you, all the better.

Then there is singing. Many people enjoy singing in the car, and your older child may too. If there are songs you both like, have at it and enjoy.

If your child is drawn to sit and explore with an instrument, this opens a wonderful opportunity to play and explore together. You don't need to know how to play anything in particular. Think of piano keys, for example, as a person having a conversation. If your child is playing three keys, one after the other, copy what they are doing and try doing it together. If you can take turns, you are creating a sort of conversation together. This can be fun and motivating, and by going back and forth you are teaching turn-taking and joint interaction.

In the chapters that follow, I will be introducing ways to build on these music experiences to help your child regulate their emotions and behaviors, expand their language abilities, and improve their social learning. As I noted before, this is a bit more difficult if your child limits where and when music can be sung or played. It's important that you find a song or a music experience or activity that you enjoy, and that you also introduce that activity in different places and at different times of the day or week. This will help your child grow in flexibility and tolerance. For example, singing a song together in the car may be enjoyable for them. When you turn the car off and get out, the child may feel that the experience needs to end, because the car is where the singing takes place. This will limit them and you. If this is the case, try continuing to hum the song as you open your door and help your child out of the car, or try talking about it being an "everywhere song." Try singing it in the kitchen or in the bathtub, and tap the rhythm out with pots and pans or bath toys. Sing with siblings or friends. The wonderful thing about music is that you can sing it or play it almost everywhere.

Music Connects Our World

As a child with autism grows, it is vital that they have as many connectors to the world as possible. Many aspects of social gatherings may be challenging for a child who is sensitive to the myriad of inputs coming in. Finding ways to enjoyably connect with others is important. Music is a pleasurable and special way to find the togetherness in our everyday lives. It is connected to classrooms, churches, home life, and social gatherings. It is a form of entertainment that gives us ways to process emotion. The more you can offer connectors that your child enjoys, the more they will feel comfortable as they learn to move through the world.

Music is Just Another Part of All of Us

When we use music to motivate, we don't need candy or treats or rewards. Music has been shown to increase endorphins (pleasure hormones) that are naturally occurring in our bodies. The most amazing thing about music is that music is the healthiest reward of all. Have you seen your child's face light up when a song comes on that they like? There it is, plain as day. What a perfect tool to work on engagement, communication, and socialization.

Think of music as a part of the human body, mind, and spirit. We all respond one way or another to music, and it is in us and all around us. Think about how many ways we hear music, think about it, and reach for it. Think about all the places it is available (everywhere!) Then think about your relationship with music and what it means to you. This will help you figure out your own comfort level in bringing it in as a tool to help you connect with your child and help your child connect to their world.

So when the day has gotten especially long or exhausting or when you just need another place to be, reach for music. The easiest tool you have is your voice, because it goes wherever you go. You always have it. Find those tunes that move you and rock you and make you want to sing and move. Then share them, because although it may be difficult sometimes to connect with your child and for your child to connect to you, there are always new places to go that you haven't gone to yet. Music may be one of them. Music is a place to begin.

CHAPTER 4
The Many Faces of Emotion

My autism makes things shine. Sometimes I think it is amazing, but sometimes it is sad when I want to be the same and talk the same and I fail. Playing the piano makes me very happy. Playing Beethoven is like your feelings—all of them—exploding.

    — Mikey Allcock, sixteen years old
    (and nonspeaking until age ten)

    (the-art-of-autism.com)

Close your eyes. Breathe. How do you feel?

Take a minute, stop your thoughts, and feel. Our emotions express themselves through our body. Is your heart beating faster? Maybe you're excited. Are your shoulders tense? You could be anxious. Do you feel as though there is a weight bringing your body down? Perhaps you're sad. Our emotions and our sensory systems are interconnected.

Have you heard anger described this way? "He was so mad that I watched as his face got red, and as his eyes narrowed, I watched his fists clench. It was almost like I could see steam coming out of his mouth!" We often describe emotion in physical terms: "I was so worried that my heart was racing!" Or "I felt so proud I thought my chest would explode." Or "You make me so happy I just want to sing!"

Beneath every human action and reaction is emotion—yes, even for people who say they are not emotional. They may not be aware of their emotions, or they don't let their emotions govern their day or their actions, but the emotions are still there. Every human moment has an emotion attached to it. It is simply who we are. It's where we live. It's how we navigate the world. It's instinctive—the dinosaur brain, the medulla oblongata, the reptile brain. Because emotions are so complex (they are physical and tied up with our thoughts, and they produce sensory responses), communicating and regulating them can be a continuous challenge. Even positive emotions that are often more socially acceptable can cause embarrassment if we feel that we are not in full control of them (for example, we may get too excited). Then there are the negative emotions that are much more difficult for us to understand, navigate, and manage, especially in social settings.

It's hard enough to understand and regulate ourselves and our own emotions, but once we have children and are responsible for another human being, their emotional states can become a big puzzle. Why are they acting that way? Why are they crying? Why are they afraid?

We are often afraid of our children's emotions, as we are often afraid of things we don't understand.

If children aren't given the tools they need to identify their emotions, they may struggle to regulate them. From the time we are infants, we intuitively begin to develop the skills to recognize the faces and perceive the emotions of those around us (babies are programmed to reference and track faces beginning as young as two months old). As children grow, they learn more about their emotions and how to manage them. They acquire these tools by watching other people, making connections, referencing parents' responses, and framing moments according to these foundational social and emotional building blocks. A child first learns to recognize their own emotions and those of others through referencing their parents, looking for facial, vocal, and physical cues from them. These cues give babies information about whether something is safe or fun and let them know and understand if they are loved and appreciated. These cues build the world of "us." As children become more sophisticated in interacting with others, these quick moments and cues tell them, "He is not interested," or "That thought is just disgusting." The movement of someone's shoulders can tell them, "She doesn't really care." All the subtleties of human interaction happen so fast and are so integrated into moment-to-moment interactions, including non-speaking interplay, that it can be difficult to know where one cue begins and the other ends. A neurotypical child maps and matches faces, emotions, and actions to those of their parents, and this mapping helps them learn the rules of socialization and how people respond to each other when things are safe or unsafe. Every step of this referencing, understanding, and being able to figure out people, emotions, and social moments helps ground a child and helps them learn that they can have some control over our world.

My Anger is Like A Train

However, a child born with autism may not be getting the same neural signals from their brain to pay attention to people at certain critical developmental milestones. Without these neural messages, the child can miss important social learning. Children on the spectrum often have difficulty not only identifying and expressing their emotions, but also regulating their emotions. This dysregulation is not a choice; it is simply a part of their neurological makeup. Sometimes they experience their emotions in extreme ways and have difficulty bringing those emotions under control. A child with autism, while having difficulty telling you what they or someone else may be feeling, can absorb the strong emotions of another person in a deeper way. They may not be able to identify what that feeling is or what to do with it. This can cause feelings of anxiety, confusion, and helplessness and may explain why many children with autism can't tolerate being in the same room as another child who is upset.

A child on the spectrum may be aware when others are emotional, anxious, or uneasy, but they often have difficulty taking this awareness to the next step, such as identifying the "what and the why" of the emotional moment. *What am I feeling? Why am I feeling this way?*

Trying to cope under duress is difficult, and prioritizing one important moment over another can lead to confusion.

Where do I look, or what do I pay attention to? Without these intuitive connections and building blocks, children with autism are left to try and figure out what is happening around them.

In addition, because a child with autism may have a heightened sensory system where sight, sound, and touch may be excruciatingly overwhelming, they may also struggle with anxiety on a regular basis. If they cannot tell you they are anxious, their anxiety can increase, and regulating a higher dose of this anxiety becomes even more challenging. Of course, this is when challenging behaviors show themselves. Children truly don't feel successful when they know they are disappointing you. If your child is experiencing a heightened sense of emotion in their bodies while at the same time experiencing extreme sensitivity to their environment, you can imagine the intensity of the experience. The lights in a room may be so bright that it's almost blinding. Their bodies may respond with anxiety (a natural response to an uncomfortable sensory experience), and because they cannot tell you exactly what is happening emotionally or physically, they work on coping and calming themselves in any way that they can. How do they do this? They may cover their ears and hum, walk back and forth, or flap their hand in front of their face so it cuts down the glare of the light and gives their bodies and mind a way to diminish the input. Matt, a teenager with autism in one of our VOICSS® groups, once expressed his trouble with regulating emotions this way: "My anger is like a train. It starts out slow but begins to go really fast really quickly, and then can't stop."

What the Feeling Feels Like

We don't just "think" emotion; we feel emotion in our bodies. It is a complex process, and most of us are usually a bit behind the learning curve on knowing how we feel all the time. When we feel a strong emotion, we are usually most aware of how our emotion feels in the body and less focused on actually labelling the emotion. For example: "I can't sit still; I don't know why I feel so edgy today." Becoming aware of our emotions is a step-by-step process, a learning curve that can be particularly abstract for a child on the spectrum. How do we help ground this concept that is hard for all of us?

The Emotion Detective

Mary is a woman in her thirties with autism in one of our weekly VOICSS® adult groups. She has high sensitivity to unpredictable sounds and loud noises. She also has difficulty waiting for an activity when people are talking too much, or communicating her anxiety when a situation feels out of control. She found that making a loud sound often will stop whatever is going on, and this gives her some of that sense of control back. Unfortunately, the rest of the group does not like this. Her worker and group home team came up with a strategy for her that they call "put it in the box." When she makes a loud noise as a way to communicate that she is startled, anxious, or having a strong feeling, they tell her to "put it in the box"—in other words, to imagine putting that strong emotion in a box and closing it up so it may feel more manageable. This technique is a way for her to self-regulate the anxiety or anger she is feeling in the moment.

Strong emotions can often take more than one step to regulate. It's difficult for anyone to go from ten (full anxiety) back down to one (a calm state) immediately when they are upset. Calming oneself is a process. What we found was that in the moment, Mary was able to calm herself using the "box technique," but only for a few minutes. When the anxiety re-surfaced, the support worker would repeat the prompt and say, "Put it in the box." However, this was a very temporary and short-lived solution. Soon after, her anxiety would come right back to the surface in the same way. Emotion has to have somewhere to go. The technique was focused on stopping the anxiety itself, not on what was causing the anxiety.

The therapist became aware that Mary began to show signs of her anxiety when they transitioned from one activity to the next. She began to help Mary communicate what caused this anxiety by giving her possible choices about when and why it surfaced, such as "when I have to wait" or "when I don't know what is coming next" or "when someone new is in the room."

The next step was solutions. This is trial and error, as always, but is worth the time. Once you can tap into the "why" of the behavior, the solution can lead to much more permanent and powerful tools for that individual. The therapist began to work with Mary on recognizing the first signs of building tension so that she could use strategies to communicate before it reached an out-of-control level. For example, the therapist asked Mary if she felt her shoulders were tense, giving her clues as to how her body may be reacting to stress. With these clues, Mary became more self-aware of when her stress was beginning to build. Catching it earlier was so much easier for her to regulate. At that point, she could identify it and ask for a break, go for a short walk, or ask for more information or help that might calm her down.

This level of detective work and support for your child takes energy and commitment up front, but in the long run, it will be much more effective because the strategies will be applicable to a range of situations as your child grows. You will be able to build on these strategies, and they will be able to learn to manage themselves much sooner and more effectively. When anyone is able to manage their own life, they gain a powerful level of sense of self.

The first step is to understand what is happening inside your body (or your child's). It's not enough to just label an emotion. We need to take it a step further and always have a physical or descriptive element that is grounded in the body. Do my shoulders feel tense? Is my breathing fast? Since everyone reacts in their own way, you may take note of what your child tends to do physically when they are having a more extreme emotion. By understanding what our bodies do when we have a strong emotion, we can use this as a way to be aware of what triggers that strong emotion and be able to identify it when it's happening.

The second step is to put an emotion word to it (meaning). In these situations, visual supports for emotion words can be very helpful for an individual on the spectrum. "When my shoulders feel tense, I might be angry or nervous."

The third step is to find a way to cope or regulate. Numbers can help gauge how strongly the emotion is felt. For example: "When I feel tense and it's a three, I can take a deep breath, but if it's an eight, I can take a break or I can ask for help." Sometimes giving an emotion a number or image helps, because there are different levels of mad, sad, or nervous. I would use different strategies at a level three than I would at a level eight or nine. Offering tools to a child to get themselves back in control is a way to regain power over their situation and their life. This is critical to all of us but is especially critical for a child on the spectrum who often feels out of control and ungrounded.

Safety in Saying It

In order for a child to feel safe identifying their emotion, they need to know that they are not being "bad" having that emotion. Often anger, anxiety, or sadness are not accepted in our society as easily as more positive emotions are, and a child may feel that they are out of control or misbehaving when these emotions surface. It's important to validate that your child may feel this way and that they can have a safe place to work on calming themselves down.

A number of years ago, we brought our program to a high school classroom in Raleigh, North Carolina. One of the students had difficulty controlling his frustration and anger. The teacher told us that when he got angry, he would often race out of the classroom and would sometimes run all the way home or to other places. They had to track him down, and it was very upsetting to all involved. We worked on the emotion section of our program, and specifically on anger, for weeks in that classroom. The therapist engaged the students in discussing and finding ways to identify when they were becoming angry or frustrated, then helped them find tools to communicate and calm themselves down. The students brainstormed and made many lists, including ideas such as "Take deep breaths," "Ask to take a break," and "Ask someone for help." One day when we came in, the teacher told us that the student had gotten angry that day, and they had expected him to run. Instead, he came up to the teacher and said, "I need you to help me calm myself down." Rather than panicking and running to gain the feeling of escape from the emotion, he realized that he himself had some control over his own emotions. He stated that he was feeling angry and that he needed help. He didn't run and instead began the process of identifying and self-regulating his emotions. This was a big transformation.

This Makes Me Feel Good

Feeling good is great, right? Yes—if we are in control of ourselves. Sometimes a child with autism may not be able to regulate their body and mind when they are excited. We can approach this the same way as other emotions. Awareness first: "My body wants to jump up and down" or "My breath is going fast!" Second, identifying the emotion: "I am feeling excited." And third, working on ways they can calm themselves: "I can take a breath" or "I need to walk." Emotions can be misinterpreted so easily, and as we grow, the words to self-advocate become extremely important. Fast forward to a work setting, where all of a sudden a young adult with autism becomes anxious and begins to pace the floor. If they can say to someone, "I am pacing because I got a bit nervous, so I might need to take a ten-minute break," this can make the difference between being able to keep their job or losing it. It can make the difference between being understood or isolated.

Then there are those feelings that are just plain good; they occur when we like what we are doing or when we like someone. Learning to recognize and verbally identify these feelings can be a wonderful avenue for a child to learn more about themselves as they identify things they feel successful doing or that comfort them or make them happy. This can help them understand how they like to spend their time and how that might connect to things they would be good at, which in turn gives them the tools to communicate that to others. As they get older, these self-awareness tools are critical to finding a quality of life, connecting to others, and functioning well in our world.

Black and White Rules in a Gray World

For black and white thinkers, which is a lot of us on the spectrum, we have to really make expectations clear. There's lots and lots of hurdles with social challenges and sensory issues, but I feel like those are all manageable if we set expectations accurately, and that's not just setting them low. I think... probably more often it's the other way, where we assume people are less capable just because they do have those challenges.

— Jonathan Chase (diagnosed with Asperger's syndrome at the age of fourteen, Jonathan is an advocate, author, and mentor to young adults on the autism spectrum)

(interview with the author, October 29, 2018)

As Chase writes, setting expectations ahead of time can help your child regulate their emotions, especially anxiety. When you take your child somewhere new, if you think they may respond with high anxiety, figure out a quick exit route in case you need it. You may need coping skills in place. They need to know that they have options in case it gets to be too much. They may also need to know in advance about different scenarios—this could involve making a list beforehand of what to expect and what may be expected of them.

Essentially, they need black and white rules. Unfortunately, the world is not as predictable as we would like—it's more gray than black and white. You can provide your child with rules and expectations, but it may be good to remind them that the reality may be different than the list and rules you discussed. If it is, however, you will be there to help.

How We Can Help

First, we must accept how much we don't know when it comes to other people's emotional reality, even that of our own children. When we accept that we really don't know fully what our child is experiencing, then we can begin the process of respectfully trying to figure out why they are reacting to a situation the way they are. This is easier said than done when we are in the middle of our day, with things to get done, dinner to be made, and maybe other siblings to pick up.

You may be feeling angry that your child is walking back and forth in the grocery store when you are trying to get home. You may feel nervous because your child is all of a sudden making loud noises and jumping in the park and you don't understand what's going on or what to do. You may be feeling embarrassed because you are taking them to their classroom and they just stopped in the hallway, put their hands on either side of their head, and began to rock, refusing to move.

None of us is a mind-reader. Understanding a child with autism often takes a great deal of patience and detective work. *Be kind to yourself.* You have a hard job. If you begin by showing patience with and compassion to yourself first, it will help bring you the patience and compassion necessary to reach out and try to understand what might be happening emotionally with your child.

In the VOICSS® method, we use specialized songs that alternate between speaking and singing in a dynamic group setting. Every week we practice working on identifying emotions, using emotion words, and finding tools for coping. Identifying emotions has to go beyond being able to point to a visual of a face showing an emotion. The child needs to be able to truly understand the emotion in themself through physical descriptions or actions.

In a Moment of Distress

Sometimes finding the cause of our own distress is like detective work, and sometimes it takes stepping back from a situation in our lives to ground ourselves and be able to identify the real emotion in the moment. Am I frustrated or sad? Sometimes emotions combine, and we strike out or react at someone with all our emotions, even if we don't mean to. For a child on the spectrum, this process must seem like so many abstract words that people seem to be presenting.

When your child is having difficulty, this can be a good opportunity to give some choices and tools to help them connect with what they may be feeling physically. In a moment of distress, tools are important. When a child is in a heightened level of emotion or melting down (this is, of course, assuming they are safe and anyone that may be around them is safe), you can try statements or questions such as:

"You seem really angry or upset right now. Am I right?" You might also follow this up with "Do you need help?"

"Should we take a break and walk a bit?"

"I can see this is hard for you—is there too much noise or too many people? Let's go somewhere quiet for a while."

When a child is having a difficult emotion, they need to feel that they are okay, that you see them and can still validate them, and that you will help them find tools to cope. In calmer moments, when your child is not in a heightened state of distress, you can then help them sort out what may be going on, starting out with their bodies.

Identify the Emotion

If your child cannot tell you what they are feeling and cannot tell you what they need to help them feel better, then where do you start? A great sentence to start with is "Do you need help?" This not only gives them words that will begin the road to self-advocacy with others, but also offers them a way to understand that they can reach outside themselves for tools to cope when they are having a hard time. If they can't respond with words, visuals or choices are helpful. A simple yes-or-no question is a great place to start.

"Do you need a break?" is also extremely helpful at times. Something is coming at the child, and they may feel the need to escape from the sensory bombardment of the moment. You can then get more specific with questions: "Are the sounds too loud?" "Are the lights too much?" "Are there too many people?" Detective work is not easy. If they can describe their experience to you, the next time will be so much easier. If you are able to identify the issue together with your child and find coping ideas together, the solution will be long-lasting, and they will feel successful in helping to manage their own behaviors.

Try to build this sentence together: "When it's too loud, I feel _____."

Work together on this sentence with a few choices at first so it doesn't seem overwhelming. If auditory language doesn't get through, visual supports such as the face with the words can be helpful. Try to add words that describe what that emotion feels like in the body. For example:

Andrew is seven years old and is playing with some Legos in his room. Your family has a few relatives for dinner, and Andrew does not want to join.

MOM: Andrew, can I help?

ANDREW: (No response.)

MOM: It's time for dinner.

ANDREW: (Does not respond but backs away and looks down.)

MOM: (Gets two visuals and sits down with Andrew.) "Are you having a hard time? "

ANDREW: (Nods his head yes.)

MOM: "Can you tell me how you feel?"

ANDREW: (No response.)

MOM: "Do you feel nervous or mad?"

ANDREW: (No response.)

MOM: (Shows Andrew the two visuals and points to each one separately as she uses the word to describe.) "Do you feel nervous or mad? Can you point to the one you feel?"

ANDREW: (Points to nervous.)

MOM: "Are there too many people?"

ANDREW: (Nods his head yes.)

At this point, my advice is to offer the child the choice to join the group later if you can. Any avenue that allows them to identify and communicate their emotion in the moment (and have it acknowledged) is more powerful than the house rules. Later, house rules of eating together can be incorporated on a night when it's just the family. Change is always harder for a child on the spectrum, so it's important to acknowledge when things are different, validate how that makes them feel, and help them feel successful in communicating their emotions, needs, and wants. Gradually, you might work on compromising on nights when there are guests, to get your child more used to the extra noise and interaction, but the goal is always to give them opportunities to advocate for themselves, leading to independence.

If you can help your child find the words for their emotions, it will help them learn how to do this in the future. Identifying how we feel is the first step to being able to regulate how we feel. If they can't match an emotion word with themselves in that moment, you may have to match a physical reaction such as "Is your body feeling too tight?" or "Is your body having a hard time being still?" Then match that to an emotion word: "Maybe you are feeling nervous."

If your child is already too distraught and in general has difficulty communicating, asking too many questions may increase their anxiety. Offering a few visuals and options might work better. Sometimes giving two options is plenty to begin with. Pick two emotions that you suspect may resonate with where your child is. If they seem to be anxious, the two that can be offered are "nervous or sad" or "nervous or mad." If they can't choose verbally, ask them to point to or pick one that shows you how they feel. Questions can be posed in this way: "Do you feel nervous, or do you feel sad? Can you show me and point?"

I Can Play How I Feel

Music is a great way to identify and understand our emotions. There is no barrier to processing emotion when listening to music. As always, the first step in sharing this with your child is to explore how music makes you feel. If you are in a place where you can close your eyes while listening to a piece of music you connect with, take a minute. Focus on how the music is making you feel. Often the first emotion word that comes to mind is a good match. Try to track where in your body you think you feel it. Do pictures or stories come to mind? Listening to music and uncovering the emotion underneath it is a very natural process. Once this is comfortable for you and you can easily find parts of a song or a whole musical piece that you can easily identify with an emotion, you are ready to try it out with your child.

Often a child on the spectrum experiences emotion more intensely. They may also experience the emotion in music they listen to more intensely. Some have described it as feeling the melody throughout their body. Some individuals on the spectrum have difficulty listening fully to the lyrics, so they focus on melody. If this is the case for your child, instrumental music might work better. A great children's musical piece that goes through different types of musical phrases and instruments to describe animals in the story is Prokofiev's *Peter and the Wolf*. This piece also expresses the characters' different emotions through musical phrases and changing of instruments. Music is very personal and very culturally different to all individuals, and what you choose to share with your child should be mutually enjoyable and make sense for you.

While listening to music, or directly afterwards, have a few visual cue cards or visual supports on a tablet or computer that represent emotions. Your child, with your help, can choose from these cues to find an emotion they may feel while listening to the music. This can help reinforce and identify what they are feeling and what the emotion is called. It's really a translation from the experience of listening to music to understanding the emotion. (See Resources for Parents, page 199, for resources for visual supports.)

Seek out age-appropriate songs that you think your child will enjoy. Search Spotify or other playlist apps to find songs that will reflect different emotions. Look for songs that talk about different emotions or that reflect different emotional states. You can use children's songs, pop songs, or classical music. We are all drawn to different types of music, and it is important that both you and your child are engaged.

If your child is able to process the lyrics while listening to songs, you might choose a fun pop song that has both, such as "Happy" by Pharrell Williams. Lyrics in songs can be both straightforward and abstract, so talking about lyrics in the song will depend on how they are presented. If a song talks about being sad but musically feels bouncy and fast, this could confuse your child. You have to know what works for your child and seek out good music tools to help them identify the specific emotion. Sweet Tweets has a great song for young children called "When I'm Feeling Sad" (search for it on YouTube). One note, though: while YouTube and other websites provide access to many video songs, keep in mind that the interaction is happening between your child and the screen. The screen will always be a magnet for attention for a child on the spectrum who tends to be a visual learner, but it is valuable to try to find time to do activities with your child where the connection is between the two of you. So looking for an audio version of songs may be more helpful.

A great time to introduce an emotion-finding activity is when you are spending quality time with your child, just being together, and no one is feeling bad or anxious. Put a song or music on that you can listen to that you know you both enjoy. Begin to use emotion words to identify a song or the different parts of a song or piece of music. If you are at home or have access to them on your phone, use visuals of emotion faces to support the emotion words. Over time, your child will get used to using these visuals to help them identify emotions.

A good verbal tool is a sentence such as "This music makes me feel _____." Give your child the visuals as choices. Another good phrase is "My body feels the music right here _____." (Give some examples such as "My shoulders rise up" or "My heart beats faster" or "I feel it all over my arms, so I must be excited!"

For very young children, using puppets along with songs can be a fun and effective way to play out emotions. Have each puppet act out a different emotion.

If you are comfortable with your own ability to sing or compose songs, sit with your child at the piano or with a guitar or drum, and make up a song that is focused on a certain emotion and how it feels when someone experiences that emotion. Sing in first person—for example, "I feel sad when _____," then take turns with your child singing the phrase. It is important to use functional lyrics that they can use anytime and anywhere. What I mean by this is that many children's songs use a lot of fun yet made-up language such as "chitty chitty bang bang," etc. A song that uses language your child can also use in real life in other places and situations will help them extend their language abilities.

Your child may have a book they like that focuses on a certain experience and emotion. If that's the case, put the book out so you both can see it, and sing it together, identifying the characters and their emotions.

The advantage to using an instrument during this activity is that it offers another level of play at your fingertips. It also offers another level of emotional experience that is much less challenging than words. Playing how you feel on an instrument goes through a different channel in the brain than having to come up with the words to describe it. The words can follow. Instruments are an easier, low-pressure way for your child to express themselves. "Can you show me how you feel on the drum?" or "How does that feeling sound on the piano? Let's play together." Your child may be willing to show you how that emotion sounds on the piano or on a drum by themselves, or you can start by playing something and seeing if they join in. The important element here is listening and taking their lead on the instrument. Let them do the talking as soon as they can, whether it is verbal, nonspeaking, or through an instrument. Music gives us a natural feedback system when it comes to emotions, whether it is a recorded song we are drawn to at a certain time of the day that can give us a clue to how we feel, or just sitting and tinkering with an instrument. It is the same for your child.

Identifying Emotion in Others

Identifying emotions can also mean identifying them in other people. If you are out with your child and another child is crying or angry, identify the emotion for them if they are not able to. Help them put a word to it. Life is our practice field, and it's better for your child to learn in real-life situations so that they can generalize the tools for future settings. If your child is particularly sensitive to another child being upset, once you identify what the other child might be feeling, remind your child they have control over their environment as well. They have someone taking care of them. If they need a break, help them give you those words, and take a break away from the situation. Then identify that it might make them upset seeing someone else upset. This puts it in a framework. The reminder words "I can help myself" are good ones. Next, offer a few ideas on how they can help themselves calm down and gain some control back.

Validate the Emotion

Singing or listening to songs that validate how someone feels is important. When we are feeling sad, having a friend just sit with us and listen rather than trying to fix whatever is going on is very comforting and validating. The same is true for your child. It is so important that they feel it's safe to be sad, angry, or nervous—emotions that people in general are uncomfortable with. Before learning how to truly manage these emotions, your child must be able to identify the emotion and know that you recognize their emotion and that they are okay to feel what they feel. If they feel accepted and safe, they will be receptive to change and growth. You can find songs that represent these emotions, or make them up with lyrics that say, "This is how I feel."

When your child is having a strong emotion, help them identify it and validate it for them. Have visual supports with you of emotion faces and words so you can reinforce the identifying process. You may be able to reference music you have shared or lyrics from those songs. While you are listening to or singing the song, pause the song and ask your child, "So how do you feel today?" If they are able to answer, then reinforce their response by saying "You feel nervous today, is that right? Thanks for letting me know." You can add supportive language, including:

- "You can do it."
- "I'm here to help. What can I do to help you right now?"
- We validate all emotions. All emotions are welcome. For example:
- "It looks to me like you feel nervous. That's okay. I will help you find ways to calm down."
- "Is this hard for you? Being with a lot of people can be hard sometimes."

- "Are you confused? That's okay. It happens to me some-times too."
- We model self-advocacy. For example:
- "What happens to your body when you are nervous? How can you help yourself relax?"
- "It's okay to feel shy. You take a break from people when you need to."
- "If you need to stop, you can use the word stop. I am here to help, but you are in charge of letting me know when you need help."

Find Solutions and Tools for Coping

Coping skills are very individual. Routine and structure are comforting to all of us when we are distraught. When our anxiety begins to rise, we may begin to spiral, going from "I am not feeling very good" to "What am I feeling?" to "Why is this happening to my body and mind?"

We don't have to panic, however, if these questions can be answered in the thought process with "Oh, I know this, this is what nervousness or anxiety feels like. I know I need to stop and breathe" and then "In and out with my breath" or "I know I need to sit and be still" or "I need to walk." Once your child has some established routines and structured coping activities, the next step is to work on giving them the tools to let others know what they need, such as being able to verbalize how they feel and what they may need in the moment to calm down.

Let Music Calm Me

Music can calm emotion very effectively. A good time to start exploring this is when your child is not upset. You might present this by asking, "What music makes your body feel calm and quiet?" If they are not sure, you can suggest, "Let's listen to some quiet music and see what we like." If you can find what seems to calm them, you can use it as a tool when they are in distress at another time. Giving your child the ability to put in earbuds or headphones with their calming music may give them a much-needed respite when they are struggling with overstimulation or anxiety.

If you are with your child and asking yourself the "what and why" question, you are halfway there. You are approaching your child with the understanding that they have their reasons for their behavior, and you may or may not be able to uncover the reasons but are going to start from the 50/50 approach: *I will meet you halfway. I will not assume that I know how to fix this behavior, but I will assume that you are able, in your own way, to tell me what you feel and what you need. I will try to give you tools to help.* Remember that when a child—with or without autism—is having a tantrum or outburst, they are feeling out of control, and underneath the behavior is fear. When anyone is out of control, it is a cry for some sort of way back. It is also a cry for structure and guidance. This can be done without shutting them down or identifying them by their negative behavior. Children absorb words such as "You are be-ing mean and whiny." What they often hear is "I am a mean and whiny person." In a child's mind, this can be a permanent way that they begin to see themselves. So when they seem out of control, you can help them back first by letting them know you are there to help and giving them reassurance that we all feel strong things sometimes.

Once you have found words to describe the situation, then you can offer tools to help your child find their way back from that emotional edge. In the moment, this may be hard, and they may need to just calm themselves in any way they can, depending on where you are and the situation you are in. If you can find a clue as to what they are feeling, however, then the next time it happens you may get to the root of the problem sooner.

Once you have been able to give or to help your child iden-tify the words and descriptions for their emotion(s), begin to use them each time you see the same responses in your child. Learning words for emotions, as well as how to express them to others and be understood, is an amazing tool for defusing otherwise confusing and overwhelming situations. If you are able to, use this emotional vocabulary during less fraught sit-uations as well. Finding solutions to manage our emotions is always easier when our physical and sensory systems are not on high alert, getting in the way of our thoughts. The best time to set up some strategies with your child is when you are having some good quiet time together.

Emotional understanding is a lifelong process for all of us. Accepting that you and your child have emotional lives that are valid and part of your everyday reality is a wonderful place to begin. An important concept to build into the foundation of our relationships with ourselves and our children is the acknowledgment that emotion is difficult for everyone and that it is a journey. The first step is always to identify what we are feeling, then to allow that feeling without judging it, and finally to find tools to help ourselves navigate those emotions.

As you can see through the exercises outlined in this chapter, music can be a wonderful tool to use to process our emotional worlds. Music is emotion and can bring in help at the most important moments when we may get stuck. When you listen to music or sing songs during your day, think about how that music may be making you feel, and enjoy how music might be able to speak to you in ways words can't. You can give this gift to your child, too. When we understand ourselves emotionally, we have the opportunity to make choices about managing those emotions. When we are able to manage our emotions, we feel in control of ourselves. When we feel in control of ourselves, we feel in control of our lives. When we feel control over our lives, we are motivated to interact with others and become a part of our day-to-day world.

CHAPTER 5
Communication is Personal

Language just gradually came in, one or two stressed words at a time. Before then, I would just scream. I couldn't talk. I couldn't get my words out. So the only way I could tell someone what I wanted was to scream. If I didn't want to wear a hat, the only way I knew to communicate was screaming and throwing it on the floor.

— Temple Grandin
(Valentine and Hamilton, 2006)

Communication—and language skills in general—are often big challenges for a child with autism. Whether they have difficulty forming and organizing their thoughts and ideas, or literally can't get their words out, life can be very frustrating when language processing areas are interrupted or impeded. We humans need language for so many things moment to moment during each day, and not having the ability to reach for the right word or thought has to be exhausting and terrifying.

Relating to each other and building a network of "others" in our lives depends wholly on communication, socialization, and understanding our emotions and those of others. All three of these areas are blended in our everyday experiences. As discussed in the previous chapter, from early childhood, we watch, compare, and integrate our tiniest social movements and language based on these blended interactive skills.

In an individual with autism, often communication, socialization, and emotional understanding may be processed in unique ways. Areas of the brain that govern communication often develop differently in a child with autism and can lead to a struggle with language. The child may have a processing issue where the brain cannot get the signal to the language area to promote speech, or if they can get words out, they may still have difficulty organizing words and concepts in a coherent way. This in turn affects their ability to socially and emotionally engage with others.

Every child has unique abilities and challenges, and it's often not obvious how much your child is understanding versus what they can express. Because a child with autism frequently doesn't catch the signals necessary to motivate them to attend to social cues and because they may have co-occurring auditory and language processing disorders, understanding social interaction can be confusing. What they hear can enter their brains as a jumble of sound that is hard for them to decipher. Auditory discrimination is the way a child recognizes differences between sounds, especially between the smallest parts of sounds in language. If your child is not able to tell the difference in language sounds in order to translate them, they most likely will have a hard time making sense and communicating words and meaning back to someone else. These disorders can be an incredible barrier to connecting with others and communicating; children with autism can miss an enormous amount of the social information and general functional information that is presented to them in everyday life.

Communicating Means Something to Me

Think about when we communicate. We usually want something, or we want to have something stop. We want a friend, or a cookie, or someone to help us do something. We want to tell a funny story and connect with others, or we want to share a thought.

The motivation factor is huge in learning. People naturally want to reach outside themselves to tell someone what they need, feel, and think, but a child with autism may need some extra support and tools to get there. Nonetheless, they have the same needs to share themself as we all do.

For a child who struggles to get their words out, communicating may not have the same appeal; the reward of using language to get what you want is nonexistent or very low if it's more work than reward to get the words to describe what you want. Finding the motivating things in your child's life that might make it more worth the effort is the trick. Having your child practice reaching outside themself is so important and so personal to avoid isolation. So, whether your child uses visual supports or an assistive device or can use words, practicing initiating the language for things they want and need is a great place to start. Going out of your way to provide motivating items, activities, and/or comfort objects is important for encouraging communication and even making it fun.

Your child might be able to interpret language being spoken to them (receptive language) but unable to organize the words and sounds to get language out (expressive language). Often a child with autism will be able to understand more information than they hear but will have difficulty telling you what they are feeling or thinking. It's important not to assume that just because your child is nonspeaking, they are not understanding language or intention around them. It can look like your child is not comprehending or hearing what you are saying, but they may be taking in a lot of information, including their environment and other people, in their own way. With the right tools, they may eventually be able to communicate more. There is no timeline. I have seen children on the spectrum make a leap in language unexpectedly when they begin to leave the preteen years and enter their teens; sometimes it's at age thirteen, and sometimes it's closer to fifteen. Everyone is different and has their own path to growth and change.

How Music Can Support Communication

Music, by its very nature, is a form of expression, and a very personal one. Music can take a person into another place where they can freely express how they are feeling in another language. It is a language that can be shared with others, but it remains one that is separate from our speaking language. It exists as a sense of expression, a form of release, and a social connection. Singing with others or playing in a band has been studied as a separate form of socializing. Making music with others demands that you synchronize your voices or instrument to become a part of one creative piece. This experience, translated into a social setting, is the basis of connecting with others in a group. Since the experience is pleasurable and yet structured, it can be a safe and enjoyable way for individuals who struggle with general socializing to have successful group experiences. A chorus or band creates a natural place of expression and togetherness. If you consider any experience you have had where you are singing or playing music with others, whether it is in church, or when you were a child in band or chorus, or at a concert where the audience is singing along with the lyrics of the band on stage—there is a social bond that links everyone together. There is no struggle as to what to say or do. The rules and structure are already in place, and it makes it easy to feel successful.

The VOICSS® method is based on this idea of people coming together to form group music experiences where the natural connection comes first from the music effortlessly. Method, technique, and practicing skills follow once this engagement has been established.

Natural Routine and Repetition

Music has a natural, built-in structure that often establishes a routine and repeats as the phrases move forward into the song. This makes songs and singing a great way to grab hold of language and practice words and phrases. For example, let's look at The Beatles song "Let it Be." Like most songs, it starts with, in musical terms, a verse. That is the opening.

Verse:
   When I find myself in times of trouble
   Mother Mary comes to me
   Speaking words of wisdom
   Let it be
   (Verse musically repeats)
   And in my hour of darkness
   She is standing there in front of me
   Speaking words of wisdom
   Let it be *(this phrase already has repeated twice)*

Chorus:
   Let it be
   Let it be
   Let it be
   Let it be
   Whisper words of wisdom
   Let it be

This song is very structured, and we get to practice the words "let it be" many times. These are safe songs to sing along to, because the melody has a very easy and repeatable structure, as do the words. For a child who has a hard time processing the structure and words of language, the melody and rhythm of songs will give them the hooks to hang their words on, as they offer natural routine and repetition for language.

Beyond the Music

Music can be used as a tool alongside language or as an alternative to speaking. Melodic and rhythmic patterns may give a child with autism a way to understand auditory information and sequencing of information. If you let go of the idea that you "can or can't sing" and just think of singing as a natural extension of speaking, you can just as easily sing a sentence instead of speaking it. If you are uncomfortable coming up with a singing phrase, use a melody line of a song you already know, such as The Beatles' "Let It Be" or "All Star" by Smash Mouth. Google "songs everyone knows," and you might be surprised how many melodies come to you. There is no right or wrong way. When your child is having difficulty processing the spoken word, give singing it a try.

There are myriad ways music can support communication. Music can prompt the language area of the brain to form words by setting up an expectation of response (see page 14 for more on this). Music can also help organize language; if your child has difficulty bringing together thoughts or sentence structure, singing the same words as a musical phrase is sometimes an easier language form for them to process. Adding music and rhythm to words gives the brain a new way of processing speech by dividing language into smaller parts. The melody and rhythm attached to the words also helps us remember the words better. Music can structure not only the mind, but also the body, through rhythm and patterns. Music can help your child focus on an activity. It can raise endorphin levels in the body that make a child feel good, which in turn can motivate them to learn.

When I formed the organization Voices Together and developed the VOICSS® model in 2006, I wanted to use music, specifically singing, as a way to support individuals who struggled with language in communicating with others. I found that using songs intermittently within conversation not only tricked their brains into response, but also helped them feel immediately successful in communicating socially. I found that setting up a space to engage and motivate through music helped individuals who had previously struggled being in a group setting. By using songs specifically created for conversation, we were able to get amazing results.

There are approaches that work on breaking down the intricacies of language and teaching them to a child that has communication difficulties. However, the problem I have seen with teaching someone conversation in small details is that it is not personally customized to the child and therefore doesn't provide them self-motivation. If you think about it, most everyday conversation is built on the motivation to reach out to someone and tell them something important or create a mutual social moment. So practicing saying random words or sentences that don't fit the child's interest or needs will most likely not get optimal results, as it will not be motivating for the child.

Contrast this with helping your child use language to help them get what they want. For example, if your child wants to go outside and play but can't fully communicate this, you might take that sentence and put it to the tune of "London Bridge is Falling Down": "I want to play outside, play outside, play outside. I want to play outside, play outside right now." If your child gets engaged with this song, try dropping a few lyrics and see if they can fill them in. For example: "I want to play outside, play outside, play_____. I want to play outside, play outside right _____" If they fill these words in, switch things up and drop different words from the middle of the sentence. Eventually, you can try prompting your child to say or sing the whole sentence. This doesn't need to happen all at once, though—it's also important that your child's attempts to communicate actually results in them getting what they want: to go outside and play. They need to see that their effort with language leads to a pleasurable and personally motivated experience.

Functional Communication Skills

Functional communication skills—skills that we integrate into our lives to help us in a practical way—allow us to meet our needs and navigate the world we live in. Since speech is a very personal thing and something we use to meet our own unique, personal needs, how can you work with your child to help them use language in the moment and at different times in their lives?

What does your child like? What are they good at? If they struggle to speak, what do you think they would tell you if they didn't have that barrier? Begin from who they are naturally. This will give them the motivation and buy-in to engage in their own growth. If they love video games, learning to say "I love playing video games" or new adjectives to describe those video games will feel more useful and personal than learning to say a random sentence like "The car is red."

If they say "video" when they want to play a game, encourage them to say the whole request: "I want to play video games" or "I like video games and want to play." What will help them down the road? You may have to fill the words in at the beginning or prompt them to say the words, but taking the extra time to expand their language will build their functional communication skills by leaps and bounds and will support their ability to become independent as they grow.

In the VOICSS® method, we use technique songs with functional language that each participant can take with them anywhere and that have a practical application in everyday life. For example, one of our songs is called "I Can Tell You." The goal of the song is to enable participants to tell others in the group something about themselves. We also sing a "Feelings Song." The sentence "How do you feel?" is a part of it, and the participants practice asking each other that question.

A number of years ago, we took our program to a high school classroom, where we sang the "Feelings Song." The teacher told us that later, one of the boys had gone out into the hallway and up to a group of high schoolers and asked, "How do you feel?" The other students answered him, and it started a conversation. This was a tool the student used to open a conversation and connect with others. We are always trying to find slang or terms that match the age of the child or student, such as "What's up?" or "Hey, how ya doin'?" Openers are a wonderful thing that can help a person ease their way into social situations.

When I Feel Safe, I Reach Outside Myself

Alexa was just a skinny little thing, maybe six years old, with big, green eyes, blonde hair, and an expression that said, "I am going to tell you about myself when I am good and ready, and not a second before." Alexa had autism and language processing delays, and when she was asked a question, there was silence as she processed it. After a long pause, she spoke very quietly in one-word responses. At the beginning of her first VOICSS® session, she sat wiggling in her chair; she was having difficulty engaging and staying in her seat. She was constantly looking around, twisting her body and shifting her eyes to look at other people in the room. When the music started, however, Alexa attended to it. She didn't move, squirm, or turn around. She seemed to absorb the sounds, the melody, and the rhythm. When the music stopped, Alexa began squirming again. She was able to process the music fully and completely, with no disruption. Language, however, did not register with her so clearly, and her understanding of the meaning of words and organization of sentences was delayed.

The music therapists decided to create a sense of safety for Alexa in order to connect with her. They invited her to participate but never forced her—they gave her simple prompts to respond to but never pushed too much. It was important that the experience stayed comfortable and enjoyable to be fully motivating for her. It was also important that Alexa felt that it was her choice to respond or not. Alexa was always acknowledged and given a place in the group, whether she took a lot of time to respond or did not respond at all. In this way, a safe place was created for her. She knew that she could participate or not and was accepted just as she was.

One day, during the "Hello Song," the music therapist prompted Alexa by asking her name. The group was accustomed to waiting for a delayed response from her. Eventually, Alexa whispered her name. The group acknowledged her response by saying "Hi" to Alexa inside the song, and the session continued. We could tell Alexa was pleased that she had responded and that the group had acknowledged her response.

Every week, the routine, music, and predictability of the songs and program seemed to calm Alexa just a little bit more. Every week, she got more used to how the music would pause, and she grew more used to being asked to respond to the group. Over time, Alexa added in the language portion to the song seamlessly, and when language was prevalent in the program, Alexa began to attend more, listen more, and respond more. She began to communicate more easily as language became a good and safe experience.

One day when she was asked her name during the song, she responded without hesitation or delay: "My name is Alexa." During the rest of the year, she lifted her head more, spoke more, smiled more, and by the end of the year had made tremendous progress. Her parents let us know how much change they had witnessed in their daughter and what a huge difference it had made in her life.

Expectation of Response

A number of years ago, I was working with private clients in my music therapy studio out of my home. One of my clients, Sean, was five years old and nonspeaking. He had dark brown hair and sharp, brown eyes, and he saw more than most people thought he did. His mother brought him to me for private music therapy sessions, hoping to encourage any sounds, words, or preverbal moments. I knew he was excited about music, as he easily came to sit beside me even though he avoided looking at me and stared straight at the piano keys. I opened up a picture songbook that his mom had told me he was familiar with: "The Wheels on the Bus."

As I started to sing and play, Sean's attention stayed on the pictures and my fingers. The first verse established the melody, pattern, and structure. When we got to the chorus at a crucial moment at the end of the phrase, "all around the _____," I dropped the last lyric of the phrase purposely. When I paused, he sang "t-t-t-t-town." His mom's mouth flew open, and tears sprang from her eyes.

Sean needed the end of the phrase to occur. His brain needed completion to the song, and even if the language signals in his brain may not have responded to a verbal sentence, his brain responded to a musical one. Over many sessions, we kept stretching Sean's ability to fill in words in songs, then interchanged those moments with language, and eventually sentences. In this way, we were able to jumpstart language for Sean. Jumpstarting language is not an unusual occurrence for music therapists, and it certainly wasn't the first time it had happened to one of my clients.

The drama of the experience does not get old, and it is stunning when it happens. That moment of expectation where the music triggered Sean's brain to fill in the missing lyric was, on the one hand, a miracle—and on the other hand, it made total sense. For a child with autism, music and language may be processed in the same hemisphere in the brain, so during a musical experience, language may be more easily accessed. Throughout the five years that I worked with Sean, he gained more and more language. From randomly prompted one-word moments, he began to fill in whole sentences and sometimes the entire song. The songs, alternating with language, helped link different processing mechanisms in his brain, and in that first year, he was able to initiate sentences on his own.

How does music set up a moment where we are ready to sing, speak, clap, tap, or fill in a missing lyric? Why is it that if you begin to sing a song that everyone knows, nine times out of ten, if you drop a lyric, they will fill it in? This is called a musical prompt. I call it an expectation of response.

How Music Prompts Us: "Pop & Drop"

Music has a language that comes with specific patterns and rules. You don't realize that you know those patterns and rules innately; they are naturally established in our brains, so we don't have to think about them when we hear music.

One of the patterns is called a scale. It's like a ruler that measures how far apart one note is from the others. We have a natural expectation mechanism in our brains to work within those natural patterns and rules. Music therapists use this natural expectation to prompt for response in different ways. In the VOICSS® method, we do this in a gradual way called "Responsive Prompting." The basic idea is to allow the child to independently respond if they are able, but build in support as they need it. Here is a breakdown of how you can do it at home with your child.

Exercise One: Expectation of Response

Think about the ABC song. We all know this song. Try singing it:

"A B C D E F G (pause)"

Did you realize that the song "Twinkle, Twinkle, Little Star" uses the same melody? Why is this melody so catchy that you can use it over and over again with different lyrics? The reason is that the distance between the notes in this song is purposeful; it abides by measurable rules of music-making. There are certain spaces between notes that we are drawn to as human beings. The musical structure we call scales makes up the language of music. Scholars have studied those scales and the meaning behind them for hundreds of years. We are naturally drawn to those particular sets of notes and the universal way they make us feel. That is why certain songs, like the ABC song, are popular with many people.

Okay, keep going...

"H I J K L M N O..."

Now stop, and pop out of the song.

Where does this song want to go, and why? It wants to land back home where it started, and you are dying to go there with it.

So drop back in: "... P."

The "P" is the same musical note as "A." It is home base, or in musical terms, the tonic. It establishes the structure, also known as the key.

Our brains have a natural expectation of response that leads us back to that "P." There are certain distances between notes that tempt us more than others. They steer us to a landing spot I call home.

Now let's sing the last part:

"Now I know my ABCs, next time won't you sing with ____."

That was mean to stop you there, right? We want to sing the last note with that lyric, and the last note brings us back to the same note we started on: the tonic, the beginning or home base of the key we started in. We always want to go back home.

So now let's use this tool to build the "expectation of response." If we want to sing that last note, then stop right before the last word "me" and see if you can get your child to fill it in. Don't be discouraged if they don't. How the brain sends signals to the language area varies from child to child. Even though your child may want to fill it in, it may not be possible for them to, and that's okay. Don't wait too long to fill it in yourself, because we don't want singing or music to be frustrating for your child. We want it to stay a positive and fun experience. If they don't fill it in, you might put your hand out, palm up, to signal for them to tap out the word on your hand. They have then intentionally communicated with you and are participating, even if they don't yet have access to language.

If singing does not prompt your child for language, that does not mean it won't in the future or that your child can't use music to socially connect with you and with others. Clapping together or playing instruments (small percussion instruments) together is building connection. It's also building imitation skills as well as social learning, such as turn-taking.

As parents, we often use this expectation of response as we sing with our baby or child. We do this naturally. What music therapists do is use that general concept as well as many other techniques and place it in purposeful ways to gain positive therapeutic outcomes.

Exercise Two: Find the Beat

Music wants you to participate. It wants you to sing, to clap, to move. It also wants you to do these things with others. So go do it—together.

Music breaks down to melody (the singable, hummable part) and rhythm (the part that makes you clap and snap and stomp your feet).

Go on a hunt with your child and "Find the Beat."

When you have a song that motivates your child, before you turn it on, say (slowly enunciating every word in an even rhythm):

"FIND"

"THE"

"BEAT."

Wait for them to give you their attention, then turn the song on.

Practice this when listening to music on your own. If you turn a song on, clap to it or count to it, tapping the beat out on your knee.

When you are in a group of people in a concert, at church, or at a rally, how is it that everyone can sway together or clap together and naturally find the beat? Music is natural and guides us to structure, and it can also guide your child to structure. Children thrive on structure. A child with autism especially craves it. The beauty of music is that it provides a way for us to have fun together while building a natural structure for language.

When you are in the car or in the kitchen cooking, listen to a song you like and say to yourself, "Find the beat," and tap it out.

A child with autism may be interested in something else while you are working hard to "find the beat." Then what?

I highly recommend purchasing a small drum. Most children love to bang on a drum. If you are having a hard time getting their attention, try sitting near them and banging out the words "Find the beat" or banging out "1-2-3." Pop and drop the last word or numeral. "Find the ____." If they still don't attend, try banging out a rhythm. If they turn around, add the words "Find the beat," turn on the song, and drum with the song. If they can't tolerate you drumming, then clap or tap together with the song. The idea is to synchronize our actions and reactions to the same experience. This practice builds "joint attention," or a way for your child to share this experience with you. This may be difficult for your child, but it is worth working towards because it helps construct a social foundation.

The draw of music is like the draw of sugar. If you find the right pocket or portal to engage, you have found gold.

CHAPTER 6

Behavior is a Story

"A person with autism will hear every sound intensely magnified. Thus, if the tone of voice is harsh or strict, they feel scared and threatened and, consequently, may inadvertently scream or even attack. Aggressive behavior is brought on by fear."

— Joao Carlos Costa, twenty-one-year-old with autism

(https://the-art-of-autism.com/favorite-quotes-about-autism-and-aspergers/)

As parents, we want our children to thrive. We want them to be successful and to go beyond where we have in life. We want them to be happy and have friends. For our children with autism, we also want to find ways for them to be part of our community and thrive independently.

As parents, we have many fears: that we won't be able to parent as well as we want, that our child won't be able to keep up in the world and will be left behind, that they will be alone or unhappy. For our children with autism, we add more specific fears: that public behavior will isolate them or us, that they may not be seen as unique but instead different and will not be loved, that they won't fit in or thrive in the world, that they won't be able to be independent.

As parents, from the moment our children are born, we are desperate to control their ability to thrive. All these fears are understandable and natural. They stem from our protective instincts. We want to control our children's ability to succeed. We want to protect them from harm and ensure their safety. We want to guard them from emotional pain and fix anything that can get in the way of their happiness. The fact that we have so little control once they are born creates the perfect petri dish for all kinds of fears to flourish and grow.

This is what I call our "fear and fix it brain." The problem with living in this part of our brain is that we have left the present and have superimposed our fear of the future right into our moment-to-moment interactions with our child. Again, all this is understandable. All parents move in and out of a "fear and fix it" brain mode from time to time; the key is to avoid living in that place all the time. If we do, it becomes the norm and our reference for everything.

If we live constantly in the "fear and fix it" part of our brains, we aren't watching or listening in the present, and we can miss the moments that could be critical to our child's growth and could give us a window into their unique experience. One can miss the "huh?" moment—the moment when we see our child do something and realize we don't know why they are doing it. When you pull out of the emotion of the moment and notice the "why" of the behavior, you are able to see things with perspective. Understanding why our children do what they are doing can lead to answers and ways to help them grow. Fear, however, leads to us assuming we already know and superimposing ways to "fix" things quickly, but because the solution isn't connected to the deeper reason they are behaving the way they are, it may not be effective in the long run.

Our fears may also lead us to take our children's actions personally. I can't tell you how many times I have heard a teacher or parent say, "He is just doing that to manipulate you!"

It's natural to feel angry when you think you have been manipulated, bamboozled, taken advantage of, or given the slip. These are feelings we all have at some time or another. If we feel manipulated, we feel that someone has broken our trust. We usually feel angry that we have lost control of the situation. "I let down my guard, and see what happened," we think. If we feel manipulated, the moment becomes about us, and we stop listening to the child.

But manipulation is also a way of getting back some control. We all manipulate when we feel we need to get something or get out of something, especially if we don't feel we can easily do so by expressing those needs. The question here is: why would your child feel the need to manipulate? Is something boring? Is it too hard for them to focus? When they are doing a specific activity, do they feel unsuccessful? Is it too late in the day and they feel tired? Does their head hurt? Can they tell you?

Behaviors always reflect that something deeper is going on. Your child is presenting certain behaviors to the world for a reason. If they have a hard time communicating with you, then it is even more important to try to understand why the behavior is happening. The behavior may reflect that they are frustrated that they cannot communicate what they want or need in the moment. The behavior might be that they see or experience their environment in a unique way. For example, they may see light as very bright and almost painful at times, so they move their hand back and forth in front of their face, which allows the light to appear gentler, which in turn may calm them. If we don't understand this, all we see is that they are flapping their hands.

There can be all kinds of reasons for behaviors. Those behaviors are stories, and if they are a problem caused by anxiety or other reasons that can be understood and addressed, the behavior will have no power or need to exist and may naturally extinguish itself as the child is able to express the emotion underneath the behavior. Once we understand, we can find common ground, compromise, and communication. We can create a bridge to coexist. Behavior is a story. Just as we are not our stories, a child with autism is not their stories. They are not a sum total of their behaviors, nor should someone define them by their behaviors. Try not to label or define your child based on behaviors that you don't like, that are difficult, or that seem outside the "norm."

Remember, these are behaviors; they are not who your child is. The behaviors are a symptom, not the core of their character.

Let's look at an example of how this works in practice.

The Emotion Underneath the Action

Chris was an eighteen-year-old in one of our adult VOICSS® groups. His mother told us that he might not be able to stay in a group setting and that we shouldn't try to engage him because it might upset him. The first day, Chris came into the room with his support worker. As usual, the group had been set up in a semicircle. There were eight young men in this group, ranging in age from nineteen to thirty-five. When Chris entered the room, they turned to look, and Chris mumbled something and sat down. The group began the first check-in song. Chris stayed for three minutes and left. The therapist did not engage him. The following week, Chris came into the room and sat in the back for about fifteen minutes. Every once in a while, he would stand and pace and mumble, and then he left.

The third week, Chris came in holding a box of earphones that he seemed to be very pleased with. As the group got started, he alternated sitting in the back with standing up and pacing. A new music therapist in training was leading the group. The usual music therapist was in the back watching but was careful not to engage Chris, as his mother had suggested. Midway through the group, Chris walked up to the therapist and started showing her his headphones. He smiled and chatted with her, then went back to his seat. He stayed for the entire group.

Watching Chris, you could see the many different manifestations of anxiety in his early behavior, and then how that anxiety gradually lessened. How do we even gauge the significant adjustments he was making with how he was taking in his environment with all the new people, sounds, and sensory stimulus? The answer is: we can't. We don't know, because we are not Chris. Chris had to feel comfortable enough with his environment to make the first move. He had to feel that he was in a safe place, that he was accepted, and that there was predictability and routine in the weekly experience so he could function without the overwhelming anxiety that can be paralyzing to many individuals with autism. He had to feel that he could have some control in his environment.

If a person is confused by what they are experiencing, there is no telling what will happen next, and the normal response will be anxiety. We are all creatures of habit and like to have predictability in our world so we know how to behave and respond in social situations. What happens to our emotional well-being when these things are disrupted? Usually, we get anxious. Sometimes we get angry or frustrated when we feel we can't get comfortable.

Since someone with autism may not be able to read the room or understand rules for a given activity, their level of anxiety will naturally become higher in an unfamiliar setting. When things are difficult for a child, teen, or adult with autism, they may use repetitive behaviors and language, nonspeaking responses, or movement as a way to channel their anxiety. To them, these behaviors are predictable, controllable, and comforting in a world that is not.

The Why of Behavior

If I am to really listen and to validate someone else and their perspective, that means I am going to take a moment to look at what they are doing (their behavior) and ask myself, "Why are they doing this?" and "What is the emotion underneath the action?" This understanding will help me accommodate this behavior and make it possible to meet them halfway.

Your child with autism may be experiencing something in the moment that you cannot understand, such as the way they are hearing sounds around them or taking in the light. They may be having thoughts that they are unable to form into words. Or they may be communicating those thoughts in ways that only they understand that defy your expectations. So, obviously, your child's experience is going to be different than yours. You are observing behavior, and your child is reacting to something that upset them. Sometimes you can guess correctly, but sometimes they may be upset about something they can't communicate that is very different from what you thought. The only way to get this information is to find out the "why" directly from your child. It's important to find a way to understand why they are doing what they are doing. Why are they responding or not responding in the moment? What could they be thinking or experiencing? Why do they seem frustrated, nervous, angry, excited, or content?

By asking these questions and not assuming that we already know, we are allowing that the child may have their own experience. We are allowing that they may have reasons that should be included in creating a solution to the situation. We can ask them in the moment, "How are you feeling?" and give them some choices if necessary. We may need to help them understand and explain their emotions or actions by breaking down the moment for them, or by giving them possible choices or options to help them tell their story.

There is always a "why."

Open the Space

I like to think of the space between two people interacting as a space that can be full of positive or negative energy. The difference between a positive or a negative interaction is the existence or nonexistence of trust. For someone with autism, being able to trust that they won't get shut down or criticized is a huge factor in their ability to grow and learn. Since everything in their worldview tends to be difficult and highly unpredictable, and they feel unsuccessful more often than they feel successful, offering a positive space where they can experience success is important. The fact that people, interactions, and events are often changeable and unpredict-able puts someone with autism at a big disadvantage; part of cultivating that trust is offering ways to make the interaction as predictable as possible.

Part of what enabled Chris to feel less anxious in the Voices Together group was the effort we made to give him choices and allow him to have some control in getting used to the situation while he tolerated all the elements at his own pace. Offering choice and control in this way builds trust and creates a safe and non-judgmental place where people feel safe and can learn and become more aware of each other. This is basic for anyone. In the VOICSS® method, we call this "open-ing the space." It's like giving breathing room to an otherwise claustrophobic moment. It's the amazing experience of being able to acknowledge a difficult or negative moment without seeming critical or judgmental. In this open space, we build time to speak, but, more importantly, to listen. We show un-conditional care by not criticizing the action or the child, and when there is a conflict or resistance, we problem-solve togeth-er. We never force, but rather help create pathways to gradually invite individuals to participate in the activity and with others. It is always, in the end, their choice. There is no right or wrong answer; we listen and acknowledge.

The goal is to acknowledge the behavior without mak-ing it the focus of what is really happening. Basically, by acknowledging the behavior without blaming or criticizing the child for it, you are saying, "I see all of you and accept all of you and realize that you have your own perspective." That's a great place for any relationship to begin. It can be a game-changer for a child to realize that you see the behavior but are not judging them for it, and, in fact, that you want to understand things from their perspective. This sends the message that although they may be struggling, you are on their side, and you will help them while they help you understand what they are experiencing.

Getting underneath the behavior is not easy, and it takes time. It is much easier to want to fix or stop the behavior itself. For example: Janie is five, and it's dinnertime. As the family sits down, Janie grabs her spoon, puts it flat on the table, and begins to spin it. Ten minutes into dinner, she hasn't eaten a bite of food but is still spinning her spoon. Her mom is concerned because it's important for her to eat, and the spinning can also be distracting to the family's conversation.

"Janie, stop that; it's crazy," her mom says. "Stop spinning the spoon and eat dinner, or no bear movie tonight."

What Janie hears and may feel is: I am crazy and I am bad, because I make Mom mad at me. I can't do anything right.

What if, instead, Janie's mom tried a different approach?

"Janie, you really like to spin that spoon, don't you? When you spin that spoon, does it make you feel good? I am going to stop the spoon so I can talk to you."

Janie's mom stops the spoon and says: "Does spinning the spoon make you feel good? Yes or no?"

"Yes," Janie says.

"I see that," Janie's mom acknowledges. "How about I hold the spoon near my plate so you can eat dinner? After you eat, I will give the spoon back."

Janie trusts that her mom will give it back, so she hands the spoon to her mom. She then eats some of her food. After a few minutes, she wants it back.

"Do you want it for a few spins, then more food?" Janie's mom asks, giving her the option to gradually be able to let go of the spoon.

Can you see the way this interaction is different and allows for a change in behavior that acknowledges the reasons for the behavior? The main core of the interaction becomes less of a power struggle and more about compromising and working together to solve the problem. Janie's mom can then implement gradual changes over time—for example, the goal may be for Janie to be able to get through the meal before spinning the spoon.

There are many different strategies you can try. You know your child, as well as what works for your household, best. The aim is to find a strategy that allows your child to keep as much control, dignity, and self-esteem as possible. Your child might have obsessions, some of which might be a strategy to help them get through a difficult situation. They are not engaging in a noisy or unwanted activity to personally annoy anyone; in the end, they want to please you.

Sometimes, if your child does not (or cannot) give up what's in their hand, counting from 3 to 1 may help. For example:

"Is it hard to let this spoon go? We are going to stop the spoon for a short while together, okay? Ready? Let's count together: three, two, and one..."

Often, they will pick up on the structure, and by the time you get to one, they will be able to stop. This technique helps teach them self-management as well.

By engaging the child to count together, you are offering a way for them to be part of the solution and helping them learn some impulse control. This may or may not work, because your child and your relationship with your child is unique, so you may have to find other inventive ways to problem-solve together while putting in the boundaries that all children need.

For example, when Janie is not distracted by the spoon or by dinner, Mom and Janie can reference a picture or video about eating together and how people like to come together to share their day and listen to each other. They can then come up with a plan (it can include visual images) that includes easy rules to follow for dinner and also allows time for interesting spinning that Janie enjoys as a compromise. Maybe it's hard for Janie to process all the talking that happens at a dinner table; looking at a picture book might work for her while also being more quiet and less distracting for others. Mom can reference the visuals or the plan if Janie forgets. Having a plan can help a child with autism who is confused by what is really expected; many of our social behaviors are not predictable or clear-cut. Though it does take longer to get underneath the issue than to stop the behavior in the moment, and this strategy may seem much more inconvenient at first, over time, its impact can be so much more positive and powerful.

Through the approach of "opening the space," you are able to increase trust. You have acknowledged that the behavior is not something your child is doing on purpose to be a bad person or to have bad behavior. You have just neutrally stated that the behavior exists and that it's okay to talk about it. You have acknowledged that there is a reason for it. This also gives power back to the child, because if there is a reason for the behavior, there will also be a solution. These words say, "I am not judging you, nor am I taking away what you are doing, but I am here to help you also be a part of the people and activities around you." This approach builds immediate trust and brings us back to the 50/50 approach: I will meet you halfway and you will meet me halfway.

Me to You

You might have to compete for attention with your child's particular repetitive motion or sound or preferred play, but if you meet them there and are able to get their attention in a fun and engaging way (a song, for example), then you have found a connector. If they are rolling on the floor with a spoon that they are flapping, roll with them. Find the connector—maybe another spoon—and play dancing spoon or touch your spoon with their spoon. If they like it and are waiting for another spoon dance, wait for them to acknowledge you by looking at you or in your direction, and then bounce in with a sound of praise, and do the spoon dance again. This positive moment of success and connection can give your child a good reason to allow you to interact inside their private play again. And you've helped them feel successful with engagement and stretched their ability to play new games with you. This reaching out from their game to "our" game is important in helping them expand their attention from the object in their hand to you *and* the object *and* the interactive game you may be able to set up. You may need to do this gradually, after just coexisting in your child's play space first for a while. The goal is to meet your child where they are and help them grow.

If a child is enjoying running back and forth with a sock instead of playing with you, a sibling, or other toys, run with them. Try to re-engage them with a new stimulant you know they like. Hold the new stimulant in your hand. See if they will trade. Sing a song about the sock and the toy in your hand. Show them and ask them if they want to play with it. Focus on engaging your child. Start from what is motivating for them, then work to grow and stretch their ability to engage and interact outside that space. Here's another example with a sock, but you can adapt it as necessary with the goal of getting your child to focus on you rather than on an inanimate object:

Your child is obsessing about a sock as they run around. You enter their space and try to quickly touch or hold the sock for a moment, long enough to gain their attention. Acknowledge what they are doing, giving them the words through speaking or singing the sentence, "You are running with that sock. You must like that sock!" If your child looks at you, you might take another sock and move it along with the first sock. Pretend to tie the two socks together and call them "silly socks." Let your child take that and run with it. Making a game of moving your child's full attention from a solitary object to you is the goal. However, it has to be done with buy-in from your child. Praise for any gradual movement is an important element in building this game. Using more than one item that attracts their attention can be very helpful. Anytime their attention comes back to you, positive praise and affection are an important reinforcement.

Attention-Getting Instruments

As discussed in earlier chapters, music can be a great way to catch and hold your child's attention. There are wonderful musical instruments that are particularly great attention-getters because of their sensory appeal, such as "Clatterpillar," a colorful percussion instrument that moves like a caterpillar, or a rain stick (the plastic ones with colorful beads inside are best for younger children). Once the sound has gotten their attention away from the sock or other object, you and your child can play these instruments together. You can hold on to one end and give them the other, while moving the instrument and singing a song with it. Again, this brings the play from "me and the object" to "us and a game."

I Can Manage My Feelings

When people talk about "behaviors," they are really talking about the actions that come from unwanted emotion. Usually that emotion is anger, frustration, or, for a child who cannot regulate their sensory systems, it is tagged as arousal from being overexcited. By giving a child tools early in their life to manage those emotions, they can use them throughout their life to defuse negative behaviors.

In the Moment

When any of us is feeling frustrated, angry, or depressed, we will go directly to our place of comfort, because we want relief from those feelings. They are uncomfortable for your child as well. Giving them tools is important, but often in the moment, it is hard for any of us to be open to trying something new, and what your child will likely need at that point is some comfort.

What can you do in the moment? As long as your child is not hurting themselves or others, giving them space to calm themselves in the moment is probably only fair, whether that is rocking, making noise, walking or moving or watching something obsessively on a screen over and over. When they have calmed down and are in a moment when you are enjoying being together, helping them discover more ways to calm themselves is important for their social growth. These tools may include taking some deep breaths, taking short breaks away from a situation, or getting some water. Hopefully, it will also include self-advocacy and communication. If they can tell you what they are feeling or experiencing, this will help them as they grow and will defuse the emotions, because they will feel heard.

Calming Music Tools: Connecting the Body & Mind

Music is very personal. Some children will gravitate towards playing an instrument or listening to music as an outlet, and some won't. For a child on the spectrum, finding comfort in listening to music when things get too much can be a wonderful tool. Obviously, instruments aren't always available, but having a small keyboard in the house can be an invitation and a way you can tell if your child has a particular interest in it. Setting up a music listening corner in their room can be a comforting space for your child to put headphones on and curl up on something comfortable. For some children, percussion instruments or small sensory instruments such as tactile egg shakers, a cabasa, or sand blocks can be calming. A company called FlagHouse offers a sensory toy called "Sound Steps." These may be good for a child that needs to be re-grounded after an upsetting event. They can move from one to the other, and the steps make sounds. See Resources for Parents, page 199, for more information on sources for sensory instruments.

Helping your child discover these instruments together can be fun and give them something to come back to when they need some comfort.

The Small Cabasa as Sensory & Self-Management Tool

See if your child can connect the idea of having control over their body to having control over their emotions. Yes, these concepts are difficult for all of us, but think about some of the repetitive actions that you may have seen your child engage in. They are making those actions happen, usually for comfort and sometimes for sensory or emotional regulation. You can offer your child an exercise that uses a small cabasa to make their actions more conscious and thus help them gain a degree of self-management.

A cabasa is a cylindrical percussion instrument with beads wrapped around it. Moving the beads against your hand or arm creates a pleasant sensory experience. Children with sensory challenges often enjoy the feel of this instrument, and it can also help bring back awareness of their body's place and ground them.

To use this tool:

Sit across from your child. Pick up the small cabasa and take their hand facing down or up. Prompt them with the following words: "Ready, set & ___ (go)!" (Before you say "go," see if your child will say the word with you.)

Place the cabasa on their arm, beads against their skin, and begin to roll it up their arm. As you roll it up, you can sing a made-up song about the instrument going up, and then sing about it coming back down. Next, add some lyrics about the breath going up and down with the cabasa; as you roll the cabasa up, sing "We are breathing in" (and model your breath going in) and as you roll the cabasa back down, sing "We are breathing out" (and model breathing out, blowing air out of your mouth). This helps the child learn to connect with their breathing and use it as a calming tool consciously. They may or may not be able to immediately make the connection between the song, the words, and taking a breath, but this is a great tool to work on over time.

If this is your first time using a cabasa, it might be difficult for your child to keep track of the sensation as well as understanding you are talking about breathing in and out. Take your time—first have your child get used to the sensation, and then later add the breathing component.

Finally, you can use the cabasa as a motivator for your child to use their breath. For example:

"Okay, let's breathe in." (Keep the cabasa still at the base of their arm as you prompt them to breathe in.) When they breathe in, you say, "Great job!" and then roll the cabasa up, singing, "The cabasa goes up, up, up, stop! Okay, breathe out, now the cabasa goes down, down, down!"

This is a wonderful tool to help learn the meaning of "up and down" and connect the body's sensation with breathing in and out.

The concept of taking a breath when we are upset can be generalized everywhere, and in a moment of stress, it can help your child immensely by giving them back some control of themselves.

Extreme Behaviors

"No one knows what it's like to be me, when you can't sit still because your legs feel like they are on fire or it feels like a hundred ants are crawling up your arms." When talking about banging her head, Carly, a fourteen-year-old girl with autism, says, "... if I don't, it feels like my body is going to explode."

> — Carly Fleischmann
>
> (2009, https://www.youtube.com/watch?v=xMBzJleeOno)

When a child with autism displays behaviors that could be harmful to themselves or to others, the first step is to protect them and/or others from injury. This is a given. The next step is, once again, to ask "why." Carly Fleischman, the child from the quote above, was nonspeaking but could type words on a computer. She explained how it felt to be her and why she banged her head on the floor (as well as other behaviors that no one could understand or explain).

Often the behavior of a child with autism stems from sensory dysregulation in the body. If your child is banging their head, it could be a sign that their system is understimulated or overstimulated. It could also signify frustration over difficulty communicating, or it could be a dysfunction of the proprioceptive system (the system that helps the body understand where it is in space). There are many reasons for this type of behavior and many good strategies and resources available to help support the child who is having difficulty. For example, weighted hats have helped some children with focus and concentration. Or you may need to pad certain areas to avoid injury while you are trying to find the reason for your child's behavior. See Resources for Parents, page 199, for more specifics on helpful materials.

Guiding Questions Can Help

So, I understand that simply asking your child why they are behaving the way they are is not going to get you to the source. Children in general struggle to understand their own emotions and reasons beneath their actions, so it is a matter of guiding them there. In Chapter Four, we discussed some good guiding questions that may help identify what your child is struggling with, such as, "Can you tell me how you feel?" or giving some choices about a few emotions you think might be happening. Then provide strategies, such as:

"Let's breathe together to calm down; then let's work on finding out why you are upset."

While uncovering what set off your child may still be a bit of a guessing game, it will get easier, especially as you find out what works to calm them down. Changing the environment, such as dimming lights or going somewhere that may be quieter, is an easier adjustment than some other areas of frustration that may not be quite as immediately fixable. However, remember that working with your child to find causes and solutions will always give you better and longer-lasting results than taking things away or threatening negative actions.

Expectations for Social Behavior

While it's important to listen, keep the interaction positive, and make sure you are giving your child time and attention to find out why they are doing what they are doing, it is also important to help them understand expectations, boundaries, and the rules of your home and society. That is just part of the parenting package, no matter what your child's challenges are. Explaining these things when children are calm and not having an emotional meltdown will always be more effective. And these are areas to navigate carefully and over time so as not to make the child feel confused or out of control with their emotions.

You Know Your Child

You know your child intuitively, better than anyone else. Still, how many times have you watched and listened, trying to imagine what it is like from their perspective? I'm sure you have tried to guess and hoped that you had it right. But sometimes, you just need to ask. Behavior is a story, and it's what's underneath the behavior that will lead to answers. This process is more about uncovering the truth than fixing the behavior.

As hard as it is for parents to accept their child as they are, this is the key to making change happen. Meet your child halfway and ask them to meet you halfway. You each have a valid perspective. Help your child engage through motivating and rewarding interactions and activities, and celebrate their successes. And don't forget to pick your battles. No one wants to live on a battlefield. You and your child might not be perfect, but you both have the ability to be superheroes at any given time. You can see this magic happen in the least expected moments.

CHAPTER 7

Social Connectors

For a lot of us on the spectrum, expectations have to be clear. If that doesn't happen, there's going to be lots and lots of hurdles that crop up. So we tell a student, "I want you to participate in class." Well, what's 'participate' mean? I saw three other kids goofing off behind the teacher's back, and so I joined them. Does that mean I'm participating?

> — Jonathan Chase (diagnosed with Asperger's syndrome at the age of fourteen, Jonathan is an advocate, author, and mentor to young adults on the autism spectrum)
>
> (interview with the author, October 29, 2018)

When I was nine, my family had a dog named Biggers (a beagle with big ears, hence the name). My dad took long walks with Biggers, but he also loved to let him out of the house on Saturday by himself. He believed that every living thing should have a bit of freedom. The problem was that Biggers didn't know what to do with that freedom. Often, we would hear that crazy beagle howling at nothing in the middle of the street or getting into someone's garbage.

One Saturday afternoon, there was a knock at the door. My dad put his newspaper down and got up to open it, revealing a tall, lanky teenager. His facial expression was flat as he held a squirming, unhappy Biggers by the collar. The teenager said, "I brought your dog home." My dad thanked him and introduced himself and our dog. He then asked our dog rescuer what his name was. The teenager told us his name was Andy. He spoke in a monotone, and I couldn't tell if he was happy to see us. Andy handed Biggers over to my dad, thanked him, and made a quick exit out the door and up the street.

The next Saturday, there was a knock at the door. My dad answered it, and there was Andy again, holding Biggers by the collar. I'm honestly not sure that Biggers was getting himself into trouble, but there he was at the door as Andy's new prize. As the dog squirmed in his grip, Andy stated in a loud and earnest voice, "Big-eeeears is home." My dad invited Andy in to sit down in the living room with him and asked if he would like something to drink. Andy accepted, and the two of them struck up a conversation. This became common on Saturdays, and that's how Andy became an official friend of our family.

I have clear memories of Andy's voice at the door, calling out in the same way, with the same inflection: "Big-eeears is home!" followed by a drink, cookies, and conversation with my dad. We didn't know it at the time, but Andy had autism. He obviously enjoyed the new friends he had made in our dog and my dad. I'm not sure what they chatted about, but I do know that their friendship was mutual and lasted for years. When I got older, I remember my dad telling me that Andy had found a job and was doing well.

Andy found a connector in our dog, Biggers, and realized he could use this connector to build a social moment into his week and bond with my dad. That connector helped provide structure. The dog, from Andy's perspective, did not belong outside by himself, so he brought him back home. Because they were neighbors, my dad and Andy both had a mutual interest in the well-being—or the shenanigans, as it were—of our dog. Conversation, as they got to know each other, built on that connection, and soon enough, my dad, Andy, and Biggers became great friends. My dad helped provide a secure, non-judgmental space in which to socialize. This weekly ritual provided rules, routines, and just enough variation to create a safe, enjoyable social experience for Andy.

My guess is that Andy was probably a loner. Knowing what I know now, a child who finds themselves left out of our social world struggles with isolation and frustration, no matter how smart they are. Andy was smart and had a unique take on life. My dad seemed to appreciate this. Andy's other strengths were that he enjoyed routine and having a purpose as our dog's new friend and protector. Most of all, Andy obviously enjoyed finding a new way to be social and make a friend. For a child on the spectrum, figuring out social rules and expectations in any of the wide array of social situations we all find ourselves in can be a challenge. Finding situations and connectors that might fit the child's unique strengths is often the key.

Andy found a way to be social on his terms. Through connecting to our dog and bringing him home, he found purpose. Animals are straightforward, direct, and nonspeaking—you can't make a verbal mistake with an animal when trying to connect. Animals and humans connect through feel, intuition, physical touch, and sound—more through intention than specific language. Words don't mean much. Dogs can be especially affectionate, making them easy connectors. Andy found that the dog gave him an opportunity to create a connection to my dad and to a social experience that was pleasant. Andy also probably felt successful at having set up a positive social exercise himself. My guess is that he probably rarely felt socially successful with peers. My dad realized that Andy may not socialize in the same way he did, but he focused on what they had in common, such as being neighbors and the enjoyment of our dog. This probably led to all kinds of interesting discussions as they got to know each other.

Expect the Unexpected

When I was growing up, we had lively conversations and debates around our dinner table on everything from politics to science to the arts to people. At our dinner table, no one person's perspective about these subjects was necessarily the "correct" one. Everyone was seen as having a unique way of thinking about and seeing the world. Differences of opinion were accepted and even encouraged. It wasn't surprising, then, that when my dad invited Andy in, they were able to find common ground. My dad was able to see outside what we consider the "social norm." He understood that the rules society created for structure and social comfort did not always work for everyone in every situation. I believe he was able to just see and accept Andy for who he was.

For a child or teen with autism, adults are often the safer and more predictable choice for social interaction. Adults can adjust to the child or teen, and they are usually more socially confident and can bring structure to interactions based on their years of experience. They are also usually more tolerant of social mistakes that may occur. Peers, on the other hand, are still struggling to understand and navigate social rules themselves and are often unsure about their own social abilities. Children and teens go through many stages of social testing, stumbling and questioning while they learn how to be social. And sometimes along the way, they can be cruel and non-inclusive.

Your child wants to connect with peers, but it is complicated for them. The myth that someone with autism does not want to make friends or connect with others is simply not true. It may be hard, and it may take more effort, but regardless of how they struggle to be social and regardless of how awkward or difficult it may be, they do want to connect with others successfully. They need and want friends, family, and a close community.

For some children on the spectrum, main struggles include understanding how to first initiate social contact, then how to understand expectations and the rules in different settings, and, finally, determining what social success looks like. All the verbal and nonspeaking cues that are instinctive for most of us are not something that a child with autism picks up. It is important for your child to know when something is not safe or when a situation is not healthy. Often, because they have difficulty picking up on nonspeaking and non-literal verbal cues, they can find themselves in unhealthy situations. There is no one answer for these situations except to be vigilant and available to your child for support. It's a big job, and you will never uncover everything and help support your child all the time. It just isn't possible. This is a part of the imperfection of parenting, and it applies to parents of all children. When you do uncover something that might be unhealthy, you can make sure they know you will help give them clarity about the situation. You can build on conversations you might have had about how we feel when things don't feel right, or offer more literal and/or visual tools to explain more abstract interactions, facial expressions, or actions. This works together with teaching your child self-advocacy tools. In the end, (following our 50/50 approach), your child is unique in how they process interactions and self-awareness of their own process should always be considered. How they express who they are to others and what they think and feel is all part of a true social interaction.

Supporting Who Your Child Is

A child with autism knows when they feel connected, when they are accepted in a social environment, and when they truly enjoy being with someone else and consider them a friend.

So how do we help make this easier? How do we use the 50/50 approach as we help bridge this social gap while working to understand a child's experience and perspective? How do we fully support who they are while helping them find tools to connect with peers? What kind of learning space is needed to encourage growth and change? Real growth and change can only happen when there is validation, motivation, structure, and routine, when a child feels safe and listened to, and when they can practice new skills in a spontaneous and natural environment.

To figure out the best ways to support your child socially, begin by asking these questions: What are your child's connections to the world? There isn't one way to socialize, nor is there a set of rules as to why or how someone will socialize. Reaching out to others to connect is a unique process varying from person to person. This isn't about fixing a situation, but about personal growth. The question is: when might your child be missing social information or opportunities that might help them navigate their lives? What is important for them in their life?

What motivates and engages your child? As their parent, you are one of their most important connections and motivators. Others are things that they might feel successful in, such as video games or sports or math. Another may be music or food or a favorite pet, like Biggers was for Andy.

Using Social Connectors with Little Ones

Young children learn through their minds, their bodies, and their senses. Music games can offer holistic methods that support your child's overall development. In early childhood, music helps children learn the sounds and meanings of words. This can support literacy later on. Lyrics can help children learn concepts. Moving to music helps a child's brain develop motor skills, and, of course, music is a direct path to emotion and in turn self-expression. Music is naturally interactive and offers a huge opportunity to help young children access some of the social cues they don't normally pick up on. This section will give ideas on how to use this powerful tool with your young child, infant to pre-school age, to help increase their understanding of themselves and the world around them.

The "Wow" Moment

The first step in building social connection is to get the "wow" moment—the moment when your child finds a good reason to connect with you in a moment of pleasure. Getting them to attend to your face or look in your direction and then giving them affirming feedback, like "Max, wow! There you are!" accompanied by big positive sounds, smiles, and compliments, will make a big difference. For some children on the spectrum, looking at someone's eyes can be painful. Following their cue on how they are comfortable attending and being with you is important. When they are very young, this comfort level can expand and change. Giving this verbal cue is acknowledging that something special happened between you and that you are pleased. Integrating these moments throughout your child's day will encourage them to reach outside themself, so they will be more apt to try again. When they want a cookie, for example, it's okay to let them work for it a little bit. If they can't ask for it, put the cookie near you or your face, and when they reach out for it, turning their attention to you and the cookie, make it a "wow" moment. In this way, you can use food or other desired objects to build their language and intentional communication. Give them the sentence ("I want a cookie") and wait to see if they give you the "I" or "I want..." or "cookie." Even if your child is nonspeaking, having them practice intentionally reaching outside themself through signing, pointing, or using visuals to engage with you for something will improve their ability to interact and increase the chance that they will gain that sense of togetherness with someone else.

Music as a Social Connector

Young children naturally attend to music. New parents often sing to their babies and toddlers, even if they may not normally feel comfortable singing in general. This music-making between you and your baby or a young child is universal; it happens around the world. The goal in music-making with your little one is always first to create an enjoyable social connection and opportunity for social play. From the beginning, you can connect and have a "wow" moment with your baby as you sing a song and help them clap their little feet together; you can wait until they have their attention on you to smile, give them praise, and connect. As they get older, begin by finding what your child seems to be interested in and expand upon it. Think of fun ways you can join in on what they seem to be attending to. If your baby responds well to music, this is an easy and fun way to connect. Here are some activities to try.

Bounce the Sound

Using sound can be a powerful tool to have fun and interact. Children make all kinds of sounds; you can turn finding sounds you can make or build on together into a fun game.

For example: If your child is saying, "ahhh-ya-ya-ya" and running around, try play-tackling them. If they stop, wait until they notice you and say, "ahh-ya-ya-ya" just like they did, then when they notice, you add "Yay!" Then let them go back to their game of runaround. Hold on to them and see if they have their attention on you. Repeat the sound they made and add the "Yay!" again. Then see if they will try and imitate the "Yay!" When they do, then let them go back to running. If they just have their attention on you and can't imitate the sound, that's okay. Don't hold on to them to the point of their frustration. This game should always remain fun. The idea is to do this until you become a part of their game.

Or, if they seem to like the sounds "ooo- eee," take those same sounds they are making and try adding another sound to it. Make it into a nice little rhythm and rhyming game: Say "ooo-eee makes you and me!" then tickle them or grab their hands and smile. Try prompting them to make the sound with you. It is important to take the cues from your child and build this interaction gradually and with their buy-in. If they are obsessed with a certain sound the way it is, build on it at a time when they are more receptive, and work it into a game between the two of you. Bounce it back and forth. If they are repeating without letting you have a turn, try saying, "My turn" or "Mommy's turn" or "Daddy's turn," or stopping the game for a moment, then starting back with you. If you have access to a rhythm beat from a keyboard, put an easy beat on and bounce the sound with a beat. You can add a clapping beat if you don't have a keyboard. Rhythm can often make sounds, words, and singing easier for your child to process, and it adds structure to a music game.

A toy microphone (available online or in toy stores) can be very fascinating for a young child. Since a child with autism may experience processing sound at a more extreme volume than another child, they may also be interested in the way they can make their own voice resonate. This can be a positive tool to expand language and socialization. If your child finds a toy microphone interesting, you can play the "bounce the sound" game with it: Make a sound into the microphone (not too loud, but loud enough to get their attention). When they look at you, smile and give them lots of positive praise. They may be interested to see the microphone up close. You can say, "Max's turn," while continuing to hold the microphone but putting it to their mouth to see if they will make a sound. Then you can say, "My turn," and repeat into the microphone the sound they made. While they are fixated on the sound, move the microphone between the two of you, giving them the chance to bounce the sound back and forth. If you have their attention, you can sing a few words of a song they know, then move the microphone over to them to continue the song midway (this is a version of the "Pop & Drop" exercise from Chapter Five). Sharing a toy microphone is also a great way to move your child's attention from an object to you. If your child is not interested in this activity initially, don't be discouraged—just keep trying different things to discern what grabs their attention.

The Sweet Spot

Since music is heard, felt, and expressed in movement by our bodies, it truly is the "sweet spot" for a young child, since they naturally take in their world through their bodies. They need to make sound, they need to move, and they need to bounce. Music creates all these experiences, so using songs that help children make sound, use words, bounce, and move are natural engagers. You can use a song that your child already connects with (like "The Itsy-Bitsy Spider" or "Five Little Ducks") to broaden their connection with you and serve as a tool for learning. You can sing the song and make the hand movements; for your child, the goal will be to attend to you and your actions and then imitate them. If they seem to like the song but are uninterested in the movements or are uninterested in watching you, try stopping for a moment, and if they look over at you, give a big smile (another "wow" moment) and start the song again. Help them make the movements together with you. Give them a lot of positive attention for their attending to you and for those special connection moments. (That positive attention may be to sing the song again.)

Melody Chat for Babies

Babies will often attend to small easy-to-sing melodies. The trick is to find a song you are comfortable with, such as "The

Itsy-Bitsy Spider" or "Twinkle, Twinkle, Little Star." Go into your own childhood library in your mind and see if you recall any songs that you can use. If not, there are many songs for toddlers on YouTube available. All children are drawn to short, easy-to-repeat melody lines. You can sing these melodies using "la, la, la" instead of lyrics if you are comfortable, or make up your own short, easy melody. Do a few "la la's" and stop. See if your baby responds by looking at you. Short, melodic phrases tend to engage the brain of a child. Think about the nursery rhymes we all know. While you are singing, play with their hands and feet in time with the melody and look for that connection. Movement with their bodies will help them integrate the experience more fully. When you get the "wow" moment, smile and give them a lot of praise. This praise communicates that this moment of togetherness will always be a good moment and one to come back to. This "la la la" language is also a way to chat with your baby while motivating them to interact back and forth with you.

To take it a step further and work on increasing language skills, switch from lyrics to using a vowel sound. Sing the song only using "oh" or "ah" and see if your child imitates the shape of your mouth.

Shaker Egg Songs

A shaker egg is a lightweight, affordable musical instrument that is the size and shape of an egg but filled with beads or seeds so it makes a noise like a child's rattle. Shaker eggs are readily available online or in music stores and are great for shaking out small, repetitive rhythm structures that are easy for all of us to latch onto. Try doing this and see if it grabs your child's attention. Adding on a small melody as you shake also can be a wonderful attention-getter. Nonsense syllables, like "Ooo-la-la, ooo-la-la" or "Da-da-da-da-do" are perfect for this game.

Position the shaker egg right by your face so your child's attention moves to you as they look and listen. If they are old enough to hold the egg and want a turn, bring in the words "my turn" and "your turn" and wait for their attention on you before handing them the egg. Sing the same little melody with the egg and see if they are catching on to your "together game." Play and have fun.

Social Connectors for 3–5 or 6–9

These fun activities below can be adapted and changed, according to the age and ability of your child.

Puppets Can Sing

Singing puppets are a wonderful way to introduce your child to a game of "guess that emotion" or a game of "let's be together." Having a puppet model first can be very engaging for a child, and they may be able to attend more easily to the puppet than to you at the beginning. Puppets are a great starting point—what begins as "you, me, and the puppet" can easily evolve to just "you and me." For a child on the spectrum, while it may be hard to look at your face, it may be easy to look at the puppet. This is safe ground; use it! One puppet can be Sally the sad face that sings a sad song, and another puppet can be Andrew the angry dinosaur. Since puppets are colorful and big motivators, these toys can model interactions, emotions, and numerous other important social moments. For example, "This is how Heather the happy turtle says 'hello' to you..." In order to connect, it's important to get into "play" mode as much as possible. Let go, and try to remember the "let's pretend" games you reached for as a child.

Rainstick Rock & Roll

This activity can include social language, such as "Let's do this together" or "my turn, your turn" or "over" to demonstrate turn-taking or handing the stick over, or calling out the cue, "Ready, set, and go" to start.

A rainstick is a hollow tube filled with seeds or beads, and when you turn it over, the beads pour down and sound like rainfall. There are clear, plastic rainsticks available, which have the added benefit of a child being able to see the beads inside. I have found this instrument almost impossible for most children to ignore. Once the beads fall through to the bottom, it is irresistible to want to turn it over to see and hear them cascade back the other way. When working with the rainstick, make sure that both you and your child are holding it so that you are doing this together and you can control the cues to turn the stick over.

You can change the words of the Beach Boys song "I Get Around" to "all fallin' down, all fallin' down, the beads are all fallin' _____ (pop and drop the last lyric "down"). The idea is to pause once the beads are all down, get your child's attention with "Ready, set, and (pause until your child says "go"), then turn the rainstick over together. In a celebratory voice, you can say "Yay!" or "Over!" or "Wow!"

You as The Fun-Giver

Follow your child—meet them on the floor (or, if they are babies, the changing table is a great spot to connect). Singing songs while moving their little feet is a great activity. If they are not looking at you, stop the song and wait for their attention to go back onto you before continuing the song and feet game. This is a great way to regain the connection. Wherever you find their interest, your job is to expand on that interest and get them to the connection, to that "wow" moment, to the place where they are not just enjoying the toy or activity but connecting you with their continued enjoyment. It's important for them to see you as their connection to a pleasurable experience. You are the important element that will lead to a fun activity and the sense of togetherness. When your child is so young, their ability to learn in every way, especially socially, is enormous, and your positive engagement and encouragement will foster this ability. See Chapter Three (page 25) for other music games and activities you can try with younger children.

Social Connectors for Older Children

Current music is important for older children, especially for teens. Music is a rite of passage and a main source of communication and culture for this age group, and it will help if your child is aware of and acclimated to new music that peers are listening to. It may give them a chance to see what they might like themselves and grab a social connector.

Sharing Music

If you are comfortable playing music or singing with your child, this can be a fun thing to do together. Or you can work on learning to play an instrument together. If this does not appeal, there are other ways to share music. You can have a family game where everyone takes turns playing a favorite song on Spotify or another streaming service. If your child can tolerate the volume at a concert, you can go to a concert of classical or popular music. If your child is very sensitive to sensory input, have some shared time in their favorite quiet space with separate headphones. Music is a wonderful activity to share.

Connectors as a Foundation

Once you find what may interest them and be their connector, a next good step would be to find a group of peers who enjoy the same thing. It might be on a playground; it might be in an orchestra or chorus; it might be in a band, a cooking class, or a sport. What is important is that your child has the experience of being with others successfully. Sometimes a more controlled social situation, such as a specially designed social group for their age, may be a good place to start. In this controlled setting, they can practice using peer strategies and being in a group successfully. A well-designed group will give them an opportunity to prepare and learn and gain confidence in a group setting. These groups are usually offered by psychologists, speech and language pathologists, music therapists, and other professionals in the field. They are usually geared to building the skills that may help your child feel successful and ideally engaged. I do believe, however, that having a natural setting for socializing, such as a group that gets together to make music, cook, or play sports, is key. A group that presents trying to learn socializing as more of an academic exercise may feel stilted or boring for your child. An environment that is motivating, authentic, and positive and that builds skills in a more natural setting, on the other hand, may be more likely to enable your child to feel success and a sense of belonging, and encourage them to continue trying to make social connections.

Connectors for Your Child
Who is Nonspeaking

There are many reasons a child may not use verbal language. It's important to assume that their ability to receive and understand information is intact and that they can connect with others fully. The activities in this chapter can also be modified for children who are nonspeaking to encourage intentional communication: pointing, using visual supports, or sign language. Using assistive technology can help them become a part of the interaction. You can adapt our "Pop & Drop" method of increasing language: if you drop a lyric, support their ability to fill in the lyric in any way they can. Encourage vocalizations by pointing to their mouth if they seem to not connect the language area with communication. Another method is to support them with the many communication devices or software systems that are available. A speech and language pathologist would be an excellent choice in helping you and your child find the best methods.

For a child who is non-speaking, music can be a wonderful alternate language for expression. You can converse through a drum by playing with turn-taking or imitation, or you can play instruments together and move to the music. Since emotion can be expressed in so many ways, verbal ability is not needed. Offering your child the ability to express themselves through musical language is very empowering.

Creating A Safe Social Place

When we feel safe, not judged, and a part of a social moment, family, or group, we feel motivated to reach outside of ourselves. We are more likely to try and communicate with others and to want to be with others. What makes a social experience for any of us feel safe?

1. When we feel that we are not being judged, ridiculed, or ignored.

2. When we feel valued.

3. When we know what is expected and how the rules work in different situations.

If we feel emotionally safe, we will be able to tolerate much more confusion as we figure out social expectations and rules. We may even feel safe enough to ask for help.

Having family members validate what your child thinks and feels is the first critical step toward them feeling safe in reaching out to socialize. When your child knows that they have a choice in some things and that they are valued for who they are, they will feel safer being in the world and learning to stretch outside their comfort zone.

Recently, I observed one of our VOICSS® groups in a high school classroom. The student sitting at the end of the semi-circle had autism and had some OCD (obsessive-compulsive disorder) tendencies. Every time someone came in or out of the classroom door, it didn't fully close. This student felt compelled to get up, cross in front of the group, and close the door. The minute he closed the door, his teacher would yell at him to sit down. This happened repeatedly (he got up to close the door, and the teacher yelled at him), and his self-esteem took a large hit. You could see his shoulders sag and his head go down. However, the minute that door would open again, he would get up again and close it. He couldn't help it; it was a compulsion. This went on for the entire hour. I am sure his teacher felt like he was deliberately misbehaving and not listening to her, but the student simply could not help his impulse—he needed the door to be closed. I am also convinced that the teacher in general had good intentions for her students, and she was just frustrated by the situation. But no student wants to feel bad about themselves over and over from a teacher yelling at them if they have the choice. Compulsions are a common part of being on the spectrum. However, they don't need to get in the way of everyday functioning. All it takes is for others around the child to provide a bit of understanding and flexibility.

This classroom was not a safe place for this student. Social communication is not easy for a child with autism, and if the child feels shut down, it will be harder to motivate them to want to try and reach outside of themselves. If we are to truly support a child with the 50/50 approach, we first acknowledge and validate their experience, then work together to find tools to help. Although I believe the teacher in this case had a difficult job and had every good intention attempting to fix the child's behavior, yelling was a negative strategy that had no lasting effect. Instead, she might have met with the student quietly beside her desk, acknowledging that she recognized that it seemed hard for him to leave that door open; in other words, show him that she understood his compulsion. Maybe having the door open caused him anxiety. The student may have experienced that when the door was left open or the bell sounded particularly loud, it was unexpected and hurt his ears. This is a common issue for individuals on the spectrum. Daily life is full of unexpected sounds, smells, and occurrences, and people with autism often have a very hard time tolerating them. Next, the teacher could make the student aware of how his actions—continuously getting up, walking across the group, then crossing again to sit back down—could be disruptive to the other students. Then, the teacher and student could problem- solve together. She could ask him, "What will help?" She could give him choices. One compromise could be to seat the student right by the door so when he needed to get up and down, it would be less disruptive to the group. Another solution could be for the student to have something he could hold and squeeze to lessen his anxiety when the door was opened.

Here's a sample step-by-step script for this situation that a parent or a teacher can use:

1. Establish and frame the student's action so they are aware of what they are doing. "I noticed you are getting up, crossing in the front of the group, and closing the door over and over every time the door is opened." Then ask, "Is it hard for you to leave it open?" or "Do you feel the need to close it?" Wait for a response of acknowledgement or an answer.

2. Next, state why this is a problem: "It may be distracting for the music therapist and your friends in the group every time you get up and sit down. What do you think?"

3. Then, work together to find a solution: "How can we solve this problem?" If he does not have an answer, you might offer a suggestion: "How about you sit near the door, and if you feel the need to close it quietly, the others won't be as disrupted. Maybe we can practice closing it quietly. Should we see if that helps?"

If a person feels listened to and validated, they will be more willing to compromise, try new things, and respond to others. Compulsions don't have quick fixes. It may be a gradual process, but in the end, the student is a part of the solution and is learning self-awareness, problem-solving, and self-management skills, all of which establish the foundation of future life skills. Acknowledging that the student is struggling with his own compulsion validates that he has a perspective and reason for his actions. By "opening the space" and including a child in the problem-solving of a difficult moment, you have created a safe space to learn socialization. As we look at our moment-to-moment interactions and ways we support someone socially, "opening the space" will help set your child up for success socially.

We can contrast this student's initial experience with Andy's experience, discussed earlier in this chapter. Andy felt safe in our house from the beginning because he was not criticized or judged. He trusted that there was a structure and routine that he could understand for his visits, and he was valued for how he expressed himself when he was with people. Andy knew that when he came to the door and brought the dog home, my dad would invite him in, and they would sit in the living room and chat. He didn't have to introduce himself or explain himself, because my dad had provided the structure.

Unfortunately, the world a child with autism enters into as an adult isn't always as positive or clear. In fact, our social world is typically unclear and very complicated. But offering children ways to connect socially from an early age helps so much; they can enter the adult world feeling like they can learn, be successful, and have positive experiences.

Favorite Toys or Interests

A child with autism will usually want to begin a conversation with their own interest. They will be often centered on their interests because interests provide a safe place, a known place, and a place that makes sense to them. As children grow, if their particular interest stays with them, they may show highly skilled intellectual abilities when it comes to learning details in their specific area of interest. Yes, you want them to be able to expand into a social arena, but it's also important to acknowledge their intelligence, talent, or deep interest in a topic.

As they get older, their interests can connect them to others or lead them to good job opportunities in the future. In any case, their self-esteem is the important element to keep intact, so how you suggest things to your child or offer a place of growth is critical.

We can begin right where the child is: with their interest. If they don't have the words to describe their interest, give them the language, such as, "I like to play with trains" or "I like to talk about trains." The particular toy train that may be their obsession is a great way to give them the verbal tool of "I want my train" or "I feel good when I have my train." Then, if you are at the park or in another public place where other children are, you could pose the question, "I wonder if that little boy likes trains." The goal is to help your child understand their own reasons for what they enjoy doing and thinking about, and as they get older, understand the idea that others have reasons and interests as well. Offering your child a question they can use with others, like "What do you like talking about or playing with?" is a good place to start. Even if the interaction is uneven or awkward, it is an interaction that they can feel successful in starting.

We can provide simple social structures for day-to-day situations, such as what is expected in a classroom or how to access certain things. Try and discuss how your child sees a situation. Brainstorm outcomes or scenarios. Taking the time to have a conversation with your child before an event is an important first step. Provide explanations such as: *This is an event where people are gathering to get to know more about each other. That means if you like playing video games, you can ask another kid there if they like video games as well. Then you can see if you like some of the same ones.*

You know your child and what they typically seem most stressed about. If they are able to tell you and discuss those things, that's great. Sometimes putting their questions or worries into words is not easy. You may give them a few things that they can hang on to, such as: *We are going to a big room that will have tables with food on them, and people will be taking a plate and helping themselves to food and drinks. There will be music playing. The people have come to talk to each other and get to know each other. We will all be together, so if you have questions, you can ask.* Other things you can discuss are:

- What are some other things you can talk about with people?
- What are some things that may happen?
- What is expected when you meet someone or walk into the event?
- Is the event going to take place in a big room or small room?
- Will it be loud or quiet?
- These are some things that may happen that are unexpected (list them).
- These things will be under your control (list them).

Limit this conversation to your child's tolerance level. Too much information can also be overwhelming. If your child is on the spectrum, they are more likely than not thinking very literally and may miss many subtle social cues. They may have to learn to ask when they don't understand or to let people know they don't understand. At the same time, you may need to accommodate them as well by explaining and being more direct.

A social framework or goal could also include talking with your child about how to make a friend. Why do I want to talk with this person? I want to get to know if they will make a good friend or acquaintance for me. I might also want to work with them together on a project. They might know things that I don't and may be able to help me build this toy Lego rocket.

Giving your child the time and space to understand their own thoughts, social anxieties, or confusion helps them gain a sense of control over their own lives as well as the understanding that everyone makes social mistakes. This way, they can feel that the social space is non-judgmental, that they will be valued, and that they have an idea of what the expectations are.

Give an Out

There was a thirty-five-year-old man in one of our adult groups who had autism and who had not been able to participate in any other group situation. He had auditory sensitivities and kept headphones with him. The first day of group, he stood near the door for the entire session, watching. This was absolutely encouraged. The music therapist chatted a bit with him and let him know that it was his choice whether and how he wanted to participate.

The next week, he came into the room and sat in the back. The following week, he came in and was offered a chair among the group in the semicircle. He took a chair but slid it back a few inches away from the others. Over the next several sessions, he made gradual progress, eventually sitting next to his peers and becoming a fully participating member of the group. He has been in this group now for four years. He found that we were a place that he could trust, and he felt safe because it was his choice to be there. He knows that if it gets to be too much, he can tell someone and either take a break or leave, and this has helped him build trust both in us and in trying new things.

The Sense of Together

From the time we are in preschool, most children learn to be able to sit together in a circle. For many of the reasons already mentioned, this may be difficult for a child with autism. That said, being able to sit together with others, feeling the sense of everyone participating and enjoying an activity together, is a very foundational social step. Sitting with others to do an activity, whether it is with one person or a group, may be a difficult concept for a child on the spectrum, but we can make it easier with music.

Try this activity as a first step: get out a drum or a pot and some wooden spoons. Sit opposite your child in a comfortable space with the drum or pot between you.

Cue your child in with "Are we ready?"

Then count to four, holding up your fingers in the air.

Put your hands on the drum and start a steady beat. After eight to twelve beats, or after you know your child is in sync with you, say, "Annnnnnnnnnd... (put your hand up and bring it down in the middle of the drum) stop!"

Ask your child if they want to count you in this time.

Begin again and take turns being the "stop." This helps your child get a sense of when you are jointly playing together and when you are stopping. This also teaches impulse control, self-regulation, and turn-taking, which are all essential to functioning within a group.

You can also put a song on top of the drumming or make different sounds on the drum, such as a rubbing sound or tapping sound.

For a toddler, you can use nursery rhymes or lullabies, like "Twinkle, Twinkle, Little Star." If your child doesn't imitate your hands with your movements, try helping them by holding their hands and moving them to the song together. "Row, Row, Row Your Boat" is perfect to do while holding your child's arms so you both can practice pretend rowing together. Bringing physical movements together while singing or playing is important for their development.

Playing music together with your child will help increase their ability to imitate, which is directly linked to their ability to access information around them on a daily basis. The song "Head, Shoulders, Knees, and Toes" is a good one for improving this skill, but if your child is not pointing to the corresponding body parts or identifying things, then you need to break this down further. They may be unable to identify where their fingers are. A good exercise is to just quickly take their fingers and lightly squeeze the tip of each finger to help them feel where they are. Then try to sing while bringing their hand to their head. Continue with the song, and when you get to the word "toes," drop the lyric and see if they will initiate the word or action to show you where their toes are.

For an older child, there are wonderful call-and-response activities that can build interactions and connections. These activities also help them feel successful initiating a sound or action.

1. Sit opposite your child with a drum, and get an easy, steady beat going.

2. With the rhythm, say "my turn," then make an easy vocalization using the word "hey" in a very simple pattern.

3. Say "your turn," and see if they can imitate your vocalization.

4. Then see if they want a turn at making up a sound or vocalization.

The Car is My Music Hub

Most parents of children between the ages of six and sixteen are driving their children around a good portion of many—if not all—afternoons from one activity to another. As a parent of a child with autism, you are most likely in the car even more and, from a younger age, taking your child to support interventions and appointments. The car can be a wonderful opportunity to create a music hub for social connection. If your child is used to turning electronics on in the car, maybe begin by having a five-minute break from the screen and playing music that you both can sing along with or just enjoy. See if you can extend that to thirty minutes or choose a specific day to be "music day." The important thing is that the music you choose for the car is music that your child really enjoys. There are all kinds of interactive games you can play while listening to music. Here are a couple:

"Sound the Instruments" and "Choosing Songs"

Music is easy in the car where there aren't as many distractions, and it can create a very special "together" time for you and your child. Put on a song or piece of music that you know your child enjoys. See if you and your child can sing along with one of the instruments in the song—for example, the drums—and make the drum sound. Next, see if you can pick out another instrument. You can decide together whether you think the music is sad or happy. Take turns deciding what song to play—this teaches sharing and turn-taking. If you are working with your child to expand their verbal initiations, give them a choice of two or three songs and ask, "Which one?" Before you start the car, you can show them visuals, or if they are able to say the first word of the title of the song, prompt them to try the whole song title. Picking a song reinforces that they can have some control of their environment as well as practicing making choices. It's a real win-win.

Music as a Social Connector

Like the spokes of a wheel, communication, socialization, and emotional development are all interconnected. Every truly socially connected moment has some form of communication and emotion attached to it. VOICSS® was formed to offer a safe space that established a motivational foundation based on this notion that all the components of our social world are interrelated and connect together to create one experience. We assume that everyone is competent and can learn. Motivation is generated by music, and conversation and interaction are practiced in an enjoyable, safe, non-judgmental, and spontaneous environment.

Music is a natural connector, because it links us together socially and emotionally and provides a way to communicate. Singing with others, or playing in a band or orchestra, is a form of joint socialization. Music creates a safe and structured place to experience a social connection with others with clear boundaries and rules. Music directly connects to our emotions, helping us experience feelings together without having to use verbal language to articulate or navigate those feelings. Music introduces new sensory input and pathways to increase many skills. There is no area of risk, and there truly is nothing to lose by trying these tools with your child. Experiencing a true social moment is all about a personal dynamic that encompasses our own social personality, our emotional state, and our ability to communicate with others. As much as you can, seek out situations where there may be natural connectors, natural interactions, and ways to jointly enjoy a moment. This is the most important path to increasing your child's social capacity.

CHAPTER 8
Self-Esteem & Self-Advocacy

Sometimes it's hard for me to get my words out, especially around people my own age. It helps when people give me choices and tell me I can do it! I also really love music, and sometimes it makes me so excited that my words pop out!

— Callie, a sixteen-year-old VOICSS®
community group participant

Several years ago, I invited a county commissioner to observe a VOICSS® session in one of our school district classrooms. The group was made up of teens in a special education classroom. Within the group were a number of teens who were nonspeaking. At the beginning of the session, after the group had sung their check-in song ("Greeting Song for Teens"), the therapist turned to the group and asked who would like to be the speaker for that day. This was a leadership role that all the teens vied for. One of the students pointed out that Michael had not had a turn as the speaker. Michael was nonspeaking. The therapist suggested that the student ask Michael, and he did. Michael did not respond right away. The therapist showed him the visual cards. One said "Yes" and the other "No." He pointed to yes. The therapist acknowledged the choice. At this point, the commissioner whispered in my ear, "I thought you said he was nonspeaking? How is he going to be the speaker?" I whispered back: "Watch what happens."

Michael proceeded to go up to the front of the group to a whiteboard with the session's schedule. The therapist handed him the eraser (he had been observing others and knew the routine), and Michael erased the check-in song that they had just completed. The therapist asked him, "Michael, what's next?" Michael pointed to the next item on the list, turned towards the group and the room with his head up and shoulders back, and gave everyone a big, proud, ear-to-ear grin. The commissioner just grinned back, and, at the end of the group session, told me that watching the session had made his day.

In the VOICSS® model, we notice success out loud and acknowledge all successes. Each participant is listened to for their perspective and validated for their response. Each participant is given time to share their experiences, needs, and ideas in their own way with the group. Every week, someone in the group becomes our "Team Leader." This role was created as a leadership position, designed to help each child, teen, or adult feel successful learning skills such as getting someone's attention, speaking so everyone can hear, and leading the group through that day's session by announcing the next activity to their peers. This position also gives them the opportunity to work on organizing their thoughts and sequencing the session. If speaking or listening is something that they are working on, this position gives them a chance to get support and be successful in communicating to their peers. These skill areas are a pathway to self-esteem. Each of our speakers is encouraged to experience this space of success.

The building blocks to learning and growing as human beings begin with a feeling of success. When we feel successful, we are motivated to build skills, and when we build skills, we gain positive feedback from others and feel purposeful in the world. We identify ourselves as successful and gain a more permanent feeling of self-esteem, which in turn motivates us to try new things and continue to grow. These building blocks to self-esteem help us grow and open doors to new experiences. Conversely, negative experiences can shut those same doors and have long-lasting effects. Helping a child, teen, or adult feel that they can accomplish things and be successful is the key to their stepping into a positive learning experience.

In our approach, self-esteem is everything. We meet individuals where they are and assume that with the right tools, they can grow and learn. Self-esteem comes from a deep feeling of worth, belonging, and validation. How do we build this in all of our children?

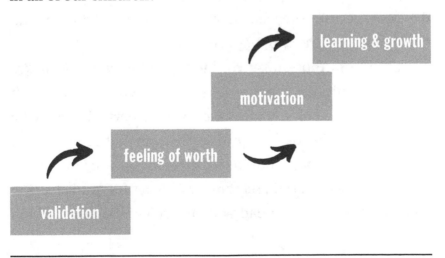

Come from Our Strengths

You know your child better than anyone. Just the fact that you are looking for information and ways to engage and help your child means you are taking those difficult extra steps to help them. It's important to give yourself credit for this and appreciate your own hard work. Also, build time and support for yourself into your day or week. Giving to yourself, whether it is making sure you have breaks, getting rest, or doing something that is just for you is so important in the bigger scheme of things. Your job as a parent is not a time-limited event; it's a forever thing. Adding in self-care strategies means that when you are with your child, you can be in a positive frame of mind. If we don't give to ourselves, we cannot give to others.

You know your child. You know what engages them and makes them smile. You know when they are doing or saying something kind, smart, or funny. You know what makes them their own person. They may have autism, but that does not define them. They are who they are first.

Lead from those positive things you know. What makes your child unique? They may be good at counting or math, noticing things, helping others, or being smart. They may be good at swimming or art or music. Hearing that someone has noticed your strengths out loud may seem obvious, but it can change your world. I still remember what a fifth-grade teacher told me about a poem I had written. I remember what a high school teacher pointed out about my abilities in a drama class. I think all of us have very specific memories of hearing our parents say something about our strengths out loud. Compliments can be very powerful.

Compliments need to be genuine, and they are better if they have some detail. What have you noticed about your child? Share this with them. Share things that genuinely impress you and that are unique to them. It can be something about their personality or something that they enjoy that they are particularly good at. It could be a part of what they are doing, such as building things out of Legos and finding just the right piece to make a very intricate structure, or putting together complicated puzzles. Maybe that makes them observant, patient, or good with details. Maybe that makes them good at building things. Try to take it one step beyond the actual toy, object, or game they are playing to identify the kinds of skills that make them successful at what they enjoy doing. It will help them understand themselves in the future and understand their strengths.

For example, instead of, "You are good at sports," how about, "I have noticed how strong your throwing arm is. You are a good pitcher!" or "I really like this drawing of the city. It looks so real that I can imagine being there. You drew all the doors and windows and details so well (or you are so good at understanding colors or shading). You are really good at art. Do you like to draw?"

When we are children, our identities are very tied into what we hear, see, and feel from others, especially our parents. We are busy building our self-esteem and identities, which are fragile and impressionable. Feedback from our environment, friends, teachers, and family in our early years help us establish the building blocks to self-esteem. As mentioned earlier, children on the spectrum often struggle with feeling success. Success in interactions and social communication is difficult for all of us, but for a child with autism, it can be a huge struggle. They are constantly trying to fit into the "norm" of the moment, especially socially. Pointing out something they excel at or have done or said that is positive may build a feeling of success in themselves, and this is critical. What we say to a child becomes their inner dialogue and story about themselves.

The more we are able to stay present with our children, the more we will be able to truly see their strengths in a real light. Though it is impossible to be present all the time, it is a good thing to aspire to. Being able to watch and listen without any preconceived ideas in the moment is a good place to start. Instead of the child being a reflection of our own fears or our own preconceived ideas of who they are supposed to be, we will be able to see them as who they are right now. Allow yourself to see their strengths as well as their challenges in a compassionate way.

VOICSS® is a specialized music therapy model that incorporates proprietary methods. The model layers in a curriculum are modified for each group and developmental level. One of the main ways we deliver curriculum is inside one of our technique songs. We call these Talking Songs™ and have modules that work on areas of learning according to age and development. When we are working to build a sense of self-awareness and to promote self-esteem, we will have certain topics that we use within these songs. The method has three main parts:

1. Brainstorming a topic

2. Alternating singing and speaking

3. Taking turns asking questions and answering

Step 1: Brainstorm the topic, with choices

Topic: What are you good at?

Chat with your child about the things they might be good at. If you need visuals, use some pictures of things that they can choose from. If they have trouble communicating, have some choices ready to discuss ahead of time so they don't feel anxious about having to come up with choices initially on their own. Get a whiteboard and write down what you both might choose so it becomes a list they can choose from. For a child who struggles to communicate, choices are always comforting; it frees them from having to initiate. Eventually, one of the goals can be to get them used to initiating and coming up with a choice comfortably and communicating it to you.

Step 2: Alternate singing and speaking

For a young child, borrow the melody of "London Bridge is Falling Down" or another melody you know and are comfortable with. You may need to find the melody of a song they may not know. Assuming they are okay with "London Bridge is Falling Down" and with you changing the lyrics, change the words to:

PARENT: I am good at lots of things, lots of things, lots of things;

I am good at lots of things, I will tell you.

Switch to speaking:

PARENT: Alex, what are you good at?

ALEX: Drawing.

PARENT: Alex, can you tell me that in a full sentence? (You may need to prompt until they get the hang of this.)

ALEX: I am good at drawing.

PARENT: Alex, you told me that you are good at drawing! I think you are good at drawing. (This model's listening and validates what they have said.)

Switch back to singing:

"I am good at lots of things, lots of things, lots of things;

I am good at lots of things, I will tell you."

Ask Alex:

"Alex, your turn to ask me. Do you need help asking?"

At this point, you can prompt Alex by giving him a few of the beginning words to see if he can pick up on how to ask the question.

PARENT: What are you good at?

ALEX: What are you good at?

PARENT: I am good at singing.

Note: You can continue this conversation a bit longer depending on age, your child's ability to communicate and tolerate language processing, and, of course, attention span.

Step 3: Take turns asking and answering questions

PARENT: Do you think that I am good at singing?

ALEX: (Pause)

PARENT: Yes or no?

ALEX: Yes.

PARENT: Me too.

PARENT: What did you say you were good at? Do you remember?

This is solidifying your child's ability to become self-aware of something they are good at, which in turn will help build confidence in telling others what they are good at and what they enjoy. It also encourages the social aspect of listening as Mom or Dad tells them something they are good at.

Keeping the Space Open

What if Alex says he is good at something that you don't think he is good at, something that you know he struggles with, or something that's more of a fantasy? Here are some examples:

ALEX: "I am good at being a superhero" or "I am good at flying."

(Closing the space) **PARENT:** "That's not true," or "No, you are not, you are a little boy and you can't fly."

(Opening the space) **PARENT:** "You are strong like a superhero" or "It would feel fun flying, wouldn't it? You are so good at imagining."

Giving Choices

Shannon was in a VOICSS® middle school classroom. The classroom had seven children, who were all in our weekly group sessions. Shannon had some limited language abilities and many sensory issues that made it difficult for her to sit still in some sessions. One particular week, the music therapist was in the middle of the session activities when Shannon jumped up and ran to the corner of the room. She looked distressed, her arms flailed, and she made sounds that sounded almost angry. She stood there, and the music therapist approached her slowly, coming face to face with her but still giving her enough space to feel safe. The therapist said, "Shannon, do you need help?"

Shannon's shoulders immediately dropped down as her stress level decreased, and she looked at the therapist, who calmly said again, "Shannon, do you need help?" Shannon nodded. The therapist asked, "Shannon, how do you feel?" Shannon just looked at her. The therapist brought out the emotion faces that identified feelings visually and with written words. To keep the situation from becoming too overwhelming, she gave Shannon three choices: nervous, angry, and tired. She asked, "Can you tell me which one you feel?" Shannon immediately pointed to nervous. The therapist validated this by saying, "Oh, so you feel nervous, is that right?" Shannon nodded. Then the therapist asked, "Is it too loud in here?" Shannon looked at the therapist. The therapist asked again, and Shannon nodded. "Do you need a break or should we sing a little more quietly?" Shannon expressed that she needed a break. She was given a break, and by being allowed this choice, she began to feel that she had some control over her situation and environment. The therapist, in turn, began to understand that sound sensitivities underlay Shannon's behavior. The therapist ultimately worked with Shannon's classroom teacher, who worked with her parents to arrange for some headphones to mute the sound. As a result, Shannon was able to sit for much longer periods of time in the group and became able to sit for the whole session every week.

When a child who normally struggles to feel success, especially a child with autism, is given choices (even if those choices are leading them to the thing that they don't necessarily want to do), we are establishing another avenue to self-esteem. A young child needs structure and to feel like they can be part of the solution.

Participation is always voluntary in our program. We offer choice as to what might help them respond and participate; however, it is always a choice. *By giving choices, we empower each child to become part of understanding what they need.* This understanding leads to their ability to advocate for what they need, and the more they are able to self-advocate, the greater their sense of control and self-esteem.

The Importance of Listening

When a child understands what they need and can communicate this need, they will feel success. They will feel listened to and heard. They will feel that they have some control over their environment and over their lives; this is especially important for individuals with autism, who often feel that they have no control over their lives and their bodies.

We all feel successful when we feel listened to. Similarly, your child wants to know that someone understands and validates how hard it is to be them. Have you ever been in a checkout line at a grocery store and the clerk looks tired and snappy? Try commenting, "Wow, it looks like you have been really busy today!" Watch their shoulders gradually begin to come down. They might change their expression into a more "I will let you in on a secret moment..." look. They may begin to tell you how nuts it's been, or about a crazy customer, or how their feet hurt. By the time you have finished your purchase, they often look calmer and will give you a smile. They have been validated, noticed in their moment of fatigue, irritation, or exhaustion. It takes the edge off. They aren't fighting against the world that doesn't see them anymore, because you saw them and supported them. This is an amazingly simple and generous tool to have.

So when your child is struggling, one of the best ways to de-escalate the situation is to ask them what's going on and to give them room to vent or tell you what they are experiencing so they feel heard. Remember, you cannot fix most things, but you can support. This takes the pressure off of you and should make it easier to give your child room to vent and express their frustration. Through a parent offering the time and space to listen, a child's self-esteem and later ability to self-advocate increases exponentially. If we want to boost our children's voices and help them become more independent, they need to feel that their voice and words will have an impact and that those words will get enough attention and support to help them be able to control their environment. It can't be a battle of wills. We can meet halfway. In other words: I will try and understand the "why" of the situation you are in, and I will let you know how to navigate the current situation of boundaries and rules.

If they feel that they have a voice and some control, they will feel safe. If they feel safe, they will be less likely to push back out of fear and anger. If they have a voice, they have the ability to learn to advocate for themselves.

Help Your Child Frame and Acknowledge Challenges

A participant in one of our first VOICSS® groups was a teen boy who loved music. Paul was tall for his age and struggled a great deal with sensory issues and language. He would usually get to the group early and sit in his chair in the semicircle, waiting for the others to arrive so we could start. There was a bathroom off of the main studio room, and when it got to be too much to wait for the others to get there, Paul would get up, go into the bathroom, and close the door so he could have quiet. This became a ritual of sorts. When he took off for the bathroom, he didn't say anything to anyone. Once everyone had arrived, he would come back in the main room, and I would ask the group for someone to count us in. We always did the count because it gave them a way to understand that this group was theirs and under their control. It also signaled the beginning of the session.

One day, I saw Paul was getting ready to get up, and I asked him, "Is it hard for you to wait?" He seemed to connect with those words and said them before he got up. The next week, we did the same thing. The following week, he took off for the bathroom, and when everyone had come and sat down, he hadn't come back yet. Then I heard him count the group in from the bathroom.

The following week, I gave him the words "I am ready to start." Eventually, Paul just told me he was ready to start. Sometimes he would say (with some help), "It is hard for me to wait." This was a real milestone for Paul. His being able to tell us what he needed and what he was feeling was more important than his being able to stay seated in the chair and behave. Knowing that it was hard for him to wait, I worked to problem-solve together with Paul and his support workers. We discussed whether getting there later may be better for him, or if bringing something to do while he waited would help. Paul communicated that it would help him if he didn't have to wait for the others to get there. As a result, Paul began coming right at the beginning of the group instead of ten to fifteen minutes early. By being part of the problem-solving, Paul became more consciously aware of his own needs and was given control over his experience. He began to use his new tools more to communicate what he wanted in the group; as a result, his self-confidence and his ability to advocate for himself increased.

If you see a challenge, you might try to frame it in a way that helps the child understand it and see it as a place of growth rather than an unchangeable part of who they are. It is so easy for all of us to create stories about our challenges that are negative and paralyzing. Like complimenting some-one out loud for their strengths, framing challenges in an empowering way to reinforce that we are all capable of grow-ing and changing as long as we are supported and encouraged will also have a positive effect on a child.

After framing a challenge this way, you can work on find-ing a solution together. Each child is different, so it may require a conversation (or many conversations) with the child to find ways to cope with this challenge. If they are in school, may-be suggest breaks and let the teacher know they need sensory breaks to walk (some early childhood classrooms have small trampolines for this purpose), or deep breaths, or an object to calm them down. There are so many exceptional teachers in classrooms teaching children with autism who have estab-lished creative strategies of all kinds to help their students. Your input and collaboration with the teacher will create con-tinuity for your child from home to school, and vice versa.

When you and your child find the solution together, your child knows they are not in the "bad" or "misbehaving" cat-egory. They know you are recognizing their challenge and also recognizing their struggle with it. They also may feel safer knowing that you are on their side and working together with them to cope. The fact that they are included in navigating their challenges will help deepen their ability to make change and deepen their sense of self. It takes longer than in-the-moment discipline, and it's not the easiest route, but it's the choice that in the end will give them the gift of self-esteem and ultimately self-advocacy.

I like to think of self-advocacy as a combination of self-awareness, communication, and taking control of one's life. We cannot make something happen for ourselves if we are not fully aware of:

- What we need
- How to communicate what we need
- How and whom to communicate it to

The core of self-advocacy begins with understanding and appreciating ourselves, our strengths, our challenges, and our purpose. These are areas that need to be supported and nurtured at a young age in order for us all to be able to nurture ourselves.

Like anything, change always happens in the small moments. The small moments eventually turn into bigger moments that change the course of our lives. Independence is made up of these small moments that turn into building blocks for personal growth. As self-awareness lays down the initial bricks, the ability to communicate grows from being motivated to telling people what we need, want, and feel. These building blocks take us a lifetime, but for someone with autism, they can mean the difference between having a life with purpose and independence and having friends and being isolated and dependent. These building blocks are the foundation of self-advocacy and help a person take control of their life.

CHAPTER 9
The Big Space:
A Place of Limitless Possibility

Years ago, we had a wonderful little girl attend one of our VOICSS® groups. She recently turned eighteen and began to participate again, this time in one of our young adult groups. Her mother and I were chatting outside of the room one day during a group session, reminiscing about how she had progressed and grown. Her mom reminded me that when she had been in the group years ago, it had taken her two to three tries to be able to participate in the group because she had so many sensory and emotional regulation issues. Once she had gotten used to all the dynamics of being in a group with other children, she really enjoyed the sessions and gained skills from them. Her mother said to me, "She has grown to want independence like any teenager, and now her father and me are trying to find a way to help her transition to a job she might enjoy." She said, "You know she is so good with remembering details and being observant. She remembers everything and notices everything. There should be a job that would benefit from these special strengths that she has." She also told me that though there had been so many people that had helped her daughter along the way, she had also received many negative messages from people and situations that limited her daughter's sense of what she could be and accomplish. She appreciated how the music therapist was exploring her strengths and the other participants' strengths in the group and encouraging and assuming that their abilities and potential were broad. The therapist built the group experience from a place of possibility rather than a place of limitations.

The Power of Intention

We naturally shape our attitude, language, and how we frame things we share in a way that reflects the assumptions we have about someone. If you assume that your child will only exist in a small, limited space with only a few options, that is what they will come to believe too. If you approach your child with the idea that they can do anything, your language will change when speaking to them. Your intention and interaction with them will change; they will exist in a framework of possibilities and options. That is what I call the "big space"—a place where limitations don't exist, and anything is possible.

To review, here are some assumptions we use as foundational principles in the VOICSS® program. You can use these as you work to help your child make gains in socio-emotional learning, communication, self- regulation, and self-esteem.

Assume that if expressive communication (what they say) is a barrier, receptive processing (what they hear and understand) is fully available.

In the VOICSS® program, we have a performance once a year during the holidays. During one of the performances, I was sitting in the audience and watching the group that was performing next come onto the stage. In the group was a ten-year-old little boy with autism who was singing happily. His mother turned to her friend next to her with tears in her eyes and said, "When he was three years old, my pediatrician told me he would never speak. Look at him up on that stage singing his heart out!"

There are all kinds of reasons why someone on the spectrum does not speak. Sometimes they are nonspeaking, and sometimes they are only nonspeaking for a portion of their lives. Sometimes they partially overcome their communication issues, and sometimes they are able to fully communicate through a computer, sign language, or words. It is better to assume that your child is understanding and capable of everything, because then when they are able to meet you in that "big space," you will have helped them get there and they will be prepared. We don't know so much on an individual basis about where each child's challenges begin and end. We also don't know where their potential is. For an individual who is fully nonspeaking, what we don't know might be more challenging. Allowing for the idea that they know a lot more than we think they know will offer them the space to grow into their full potential.

If we assume that they are understanding much more than they can tell us, then we need to be willing to watch them, listen to them, and help them interpret the world the best that they can. We need to assume that given the right tools, they will be able to let us know where they are struggling and what is engaging to them, and why. If we can't figure it out right away, it just means we don't have the right tools—yet.

Assume that behavior has a personal and valid source, and the source (the why) is the key.

There is always emotion underneath the story. We have talked about how we all have stories and we all have emotions. Whether a child is able to share them or not, assume that there are personal reasons for why they do what they do. There are reasons for their behaviors that are fully unique to their personality, their challenges, and sometimes their strengths. These reasons are definitely reactions to what the world throws their way.

For a child with autism, the unpredictable nature of the world must seem like one of those video games where things keep popping out of the corners of the screen and noises and explosions randomly take place. Give your child the benefit of the doubt and assume they have a reason that they are feeling the way that they do. Sometimes it takes time to figure out the reason for your child's behavior and validate it then work to solve the issue; as I said earlier in the book, sometimes this is the harder path to walk. But if you go for the quick fix, it will only tackle the surface-level issues. Your child needs to be a part of the process along with you. They need to know they have the ability to learn and understand themselves.

The source of behavior is the key. Once the source is identified, you and your child will feel pride in and ownership over the tools that you are able to develop. The assumption is that your child is capable and can be a part of finding the solutions to their challenges. A comment such as "I know you are working hard to calm yourself down" will reinforce that you believe that they are trying to help themselves and that you know they can do it if they, too, believe in themselves. This message will go deeper and last longer and will become a part of how the child thinks of themselves. These reinforcing messages and actions are the ones that last.

Assume your child wants to connect with other people and other children and make friends.

In my private practice, I worked with a wonderful teenage boy named Jake for a few years. He was very tall and built like a football player. He had limited verbal language and struggled with many sensory issues. However, he loved music, and we had struck up quite a bond over the years. I didn't see him for almost a year, and one day I happened to be at a neighborhood church for an event. Jake saw me come in, and as I sat down he made his way to the row of chairs behind me, then managed to climb over the row, and plopped right next to me, grinning and pulling into himself, with both hands on the sides of his head. I knew immediately that this was his way of saying, "I am so glad to see you!" Connections are important to all of us.

If we assume that someone with autism feels connections and wants friends like anyone else, we can better understand the social signals they give us. If you assume that your child is a social being driven by emotions (as we all are) and that they want to feel successful reaching out and connecting with others, then we should assume that they have many levels of understanding and ability to appreciate a social connection. They might just need some tools or opportunities to express themselves so they are understood. They also might social-ize their own way; if we are truly putting in place the 50/50 approach, we see them and appreciate them for who they are and how they interact with the world. They may be over-whelmed by all kinds of thoughts, sounds, lights, and other sensory input at any given moment, and this input may get in their way, but underneath all the noise is a child that has the same need to communicate, socialize, and share their emo-tional states with others as the rest of us. They may be social in ways that only make sense to them in the moment; they may not be able to always tell you how they feel; and they may have difficulty with language. That being said, all of us are born into this world as a part of a family, community, and the bigger world. We are all born with different needs and perspec-tive. We need to help each other bridge those gaps that might exist and invite each other to be a part of the social fabric that makes up our day-to-day lives. To assume that we all want to "belong" and participate is a good place to start.

Assume your child can tell you how they feel.

There are a million little ways that what we think and who we are come through in our language, intentions, and interactions with others. We are only aware of a portion of them. The rest of the time, we express ourselves in so many small and fast-moving gestures, actions, expressions, and words that we are not aware of. It's the way we might say something without being aware of the way we said it. It's the way we might frame a subject, request, or question. Mostly, it's the way we are known through the people we are closest to.

We let others know how we feel through many ways besides words. It can be touch or the gestures and actions listed above. If your child is having a hard time letting you and others know how they are feeling, they also may need another way besides words to get those thoughts out. Tools such as visuals, songs, or developing new tools and practicing them can be very helpful. If we assume that they are able to do this, we can add intentional communication to the mix. Intentions can be very powerful. If your child can learn to point to or choose an emotion that may match how they are feeling, they are reaching out to communicate with you.

Part of this process is assuming that the child is going to choose the emotion that actually matches their feelings. Even if it takes them a while to understand the process of matching a face or emotion word to how they are feeling, they will eventually become good at picking the correct one through practice if that practice is backed up by your belief in them and their abilities. Faith in the process is powerful. Faith in the person is magic.

Assume your child wants to please you.

All children naturally want to please their parents. They want your encouragement and love, and they build their inner dialogue partly on your attitude, words, and interactions with them. Although this can be daunting as a parent, it's also such an honor. You have an opportunity to help them build the self-esteem and foundation that they will need to push through a difficult world. It's also never too late to change the message. You are the messenger, and children are resilient.

Approach your child with positive assumptions about their capabilities and motivations.

If you believe that your child has the ability to learn tools to manage their behaviors, then you can more easily begin the process of helping them gain those tools. Let's just assume that your child is already at the top of the mountain and you can see them standing with their arms out and face tilted up towards the sun, beaming. You can see their success because you can envision them on top of that mountain. You can then set goals and break down the steps required in order to get there. If you see no limits because you are operating from that "big space," then you will meet your child where they are and give them steps that will make sense for them.

It all begins by being able to see them there at the top of that mountain. If you assume that your child can calm themselves down when they are agitated, you will begin by trying to find out why they are feeling this way and help them become aware of why they are feeling this way. Once you find out the cause, you can then figure out what might help calm them down and get back in control. They need to be a part of the discussion and solution. Your taking time as a parent to uncover the source of the agitation and working together with your child toward a solution speaks volumes about your ability to assume that they can.

Assume that your child, if given the opportunity and tools, is capable of directing their own life.

I recently observed a classroom VOICSS® group in a high school. This group was focused on transition skills—skills that would help the young people as they moved from high school into independence in their communities. They had been spending weeks talking about what strengths they had as individuals. On this day, they were discussing what jobs would interest them and connecting their strengths with possible job opportunities. Three different boys were fascinated with bus driving. They all decided that they wanted to be bus drivers. The music therapist then guided the discussion to what strengths someone would need to be a bus driver. They started listing traits such as friendly and attentive. None of these boys were signed up for Drivers Ed, and they may or may not ever learn to drive. At this point, a parent or teacher could easily validate their interest in bus driving while brainstorming what other possible jobs they could consider based on their strengths. This approach meets them where they are while offering some tools to help them grow and envision all possibilities.

If you believe that your child can tell you what is important to them, what they love to do, and what is hard for them, they likely will, because you have created the big space for them where anything is possible. By doing so, you give them the space and possibly some tools to help them naturally tell you what they want and need. If you believe someone has something important to say, you will wait for a response. If they need a little time or support to get there, you will give it.

The Three-Way Dance

We are dynamic. Being human naturally means that we are a blend of our emotions, our social interactions, and our language and communications with each other. In this three-way dance, socialization, communication, and emotional states become one blended, complex experience.

I developed the VOICSS® method because I felt that the areas of communication, socialization, and emotional expression could not be looked at as separate entities. They are completely interactive, and they exist in the same space. Teaching a child how to say, "I want a cookie," for example, cannot be just about the words. We can't separate the fact that when they later ask for that cookie, they are also engaging in an interaction. After they get the cookie, they may feel proud that they asked, or they may feel happy that they got a treat, or they may feel disappointed that they had to wait. In this small moment, we see social interaction, communication, and emotional expression happening all at the same time.

This three-way dance might seem daunting, but it really opens up opportunity. Every moment offers an opportunity for awareness and a feeling of success as a child learns to communicate in the social and emotional world we live in. When I developed the ideas behind the VOICSS® method, it occurred to me that the best place to gain these tools to communicate and connect was in a natural social setting, where all three aspects of our interactions, communication/social understanding, and emotional understanding could be acknowledged, shared, developed, and practiced in a fun, safe, and interactive peer group.

So, when you are with your child and you want to help them connect with you or others in their world, start from the idea of the big space. Imagine what that big space looks like for your child. It takes into account the many sides of behavior, communication, emotion, and socialization. It takes into account that underneath behavior lies emotion(s), that emotion(s) cannot always be communicated, and that true motivation for communicating and making a social connection can come from something that we don't expect and can bring about amazing results.

Of all the skills discussed in this book, I believe self-esteem is most important. When we offer our children a big space from the time they are born, we are telling them in our own way that we believe they are capable and can reach for anything. Out of that big space comes the ability to build self-esteem. Out of self-esteem comes the motivation within the child to do everything and anything. When they feel good about who they are, they can allow themselves to grow and learn, even when it's hard work. When they feel good about themselves, they are willing to reach out to others and test their limits and abilities. Out of self-esteem comes self-love, which in turn will allow them to love others.

Afterword: For Parents

Life is constant movement and change. Just when we think we have nailed it down, something yanks that nail out and we are left to scramble for glue. Life is imperfection. We are imperfect, but there can be perfect moments. Your child can have perfect moments. You as a parent have a difficult job. Your job will change, and it will ask you to accept imperfection and embrace compassion, first for yourself and then for your child.

You are doing a good job. The fact that you picked up this book tells me you are reaching outside yourself for ways to understand your child better. Try to take a moment and be kind to yourself as a parent.

I am a parent and have been working with parents for over thirty years, and I have seen parents, families, and marriages crushed because they have a child with autism. I have also seen parents, families, and marriages thrive and parents become larger-than-life advocates and supporters against all odds, not only for their child, but also other families and children on the spectrum.

In the end, one of the biggest challenges is being able to be present with your child, whatever the situation. Even if there are only a few moments like this, give yourself support and credit. Your feeling of success will fuel the next moment, and all those moments will bring you closer to feeling success together, connecting together, and having the strength and joy to take on the future.

From a Child

Us kids with autism would like you to watch out for us—meaning, please never give up on us. The reason I say 'watch out for us' is that we can be made stronger just by the fact you're watching. Just going by how we respond, it's difficult for you to tell if we've understood what you're saying or not. And often we still can't do something however often you've shown us how to do it.

That's just the way we are. On our own we simply don't know how to get things done the same way you do them. But, like everyone else, we want to do the best we possibly can. When we sense you've given up on us it makes us feel miserable. So please keep helping us, through to the end.

— Naoki Higashida

(excerpt from *The Reason I Jump: The Inner Voice of a Thirteen-Year-Old Boy with Autism*) (2007)

Resources for Parents

The resources in this section include books and articles that may be helpful for parents and professionals exploring autism, music, and language. I have also included some of many great books, articles, and TED talks by individuals *with* autism—who better to help us all understand autism?

The Songbooks and Products for Parents heading includes resources for the music-related products I talk about in the book, followed by some websites that offer general resources for parents of children with autism.

Books

Avila, Barbara R. *Seeing Autism: Connection through Understanding*. Welches, OR: Synergy Autism Center, 2021.

Ball, James. *Early Intervention and Autism: Real-Life Questions, Real-Life Answers*. Arlington, TX: Future Horizons, Inc., 2008.

Biel, Lindsey, and Nancy Peske. *Raising a Sensory Smart Child: The Definitive Handbook for Helping Your Child with Sensory Processing Issues*. New York: Penguin Books, 2009.

Bonker, Elizabeth M., and Virginia G. Breen. *I Am in Here: The Journey of a Child with Autism Who Cannot Speak but Finds Her Voice*. Grand Rapids: Revell, 2011.

Chase, Jonathan. *From Surviving to Thriving: Classroom Accommodations for Students on the Autism Spectrum*. Portland: Out of the Bubble Publishing, 2016.

Donovan, John, and Caren Zucker. *In a Different Key: The Story of Autism*. New York: Penguin Random House LLC, 2016.

Grandin, Temple, and Margaret M. Scariano. *Emergence: Labeled Autistic*. New York: Grand Central Publishing, 1996.

Grandin, Temple, and Richard Panek. *The Autistic Brain: Thinking Across the Spectrum*. New York, NY: Houghton Mifflin Harcourt, 2013.

Higashida, Naoki. *The Reason I Jump: The Inner Voice of a Thirteen-Year-Old Boy with Autism*. New York: Random House Publishing Group, 2007.

Kedar, Ido. *Ido in Autismland: Climbing Out of Autism's Silent Prison*. Sharon Kedar and Amazon Digital Services, LLC, 2012.

Kedar, Ido. *In Two Worlds*. Houston: Double Buck Publishing, LLC, 2018.

Levitin, Daniel J. *This Is Your Brain on Music: The Science of a Human Obsession*. New York: Dutton, 2006.

Ockelford, Adam. *Comparing Notes: How We Make Sense of Music*. London: Profile Books Ltd., 2017.

Ockelford, Adam. Music, *Language and Autism: Exceptional Strategies for Exceptional Minds*. London: Jessica Kingsley Publishers, 2013.

Patel, Aniruddh D. *Music, Language, and the Brain*. New York: Oxford University Press, 2008.

Prizant, Barry M., and Tom Fields-Meyer. *Uniquely Human: A Different Way of Seeing Autism*. New York: Simon & Schuster Paperbacks, 2015.

Rodgers J. Sally and Geraldine Dawson. *Early Start Denver Model for Young Children with Autism: Promoting Language, Learning, and Engagement*. New York: The Guilford Press, 2010

Sacks, Oliver. *Musicophilia: Tales of Music and the Brain*. New York: Vintage Books, 2007.

Suskind, Ron. 2014. *Life, Animated*. Glendale: Kingswell.

Tammet, Daniel. 2006. *Born on a Blue Day: Inside the Extraordinary Mind of an Autistic Savant*. New York: Free Press.

Zald, David H., and Robert J. Zatorre. "Music." In *Neurobiology of Sensation and Reward*, edited by Jay A. Gottfried. Boca Raton: CRC Press/Taylor & Francis, 2011.

Videos and TED Talks

Chase, Jonathan. "Music as a Window into the Autistic Mind." YouTube. November 17, 2014. TEDx Talks, 11:33. https://youtu.be/MxxUhW7d8yI.

Fleischmann, Carly. "Autistic Teen Finds Inner Voice." YouTube. August 18, 2009. Youtube video, 9:51. https://youtu.be/a1uPf5O-on0.

Grandin, Temple. "The World Needs All Kinds of Minds." YouTube. February 24, 2010. TED, 19:43. https://youtu.be/fn_9f5x0f1Q.

Journal Articles and Online Resources

Asenova, I. V. "Lateral Preferences in Autistic Children with Severe Language Impairment." *Procedia Social and Behavioral Sciences* 217 (2016): 84–91. Doi: 10.1016/j.sbspro.2016.02.032.

Callan, Daniel E., Vassiliy Tsytsarev, Takashi Hanakawa, Akiko M. Callan, Maya Katsuhara, Hidenao Fukuyama, and Robert Turner. "Song and Speech: Brain Regions Involved with Perception and Covert Production." *NeuroImage* 31 (2006): 1327–1342. Doi: 10.1016/j.neuroimage.2006.01.036.

Carpente, John. "Investigating the Effectiveness of a Developmental, Individual Difference, Relationship-Based (DIR) Improvisational Music Therapy Program on Social Communication for Children with Autism Spectrum Disorder." *Music Therapy Perspectives* 35 (2017): 160–174. Doi: 10.1093/mtp/miw013.

Chanda, M.L. and Daniel J. Levitin. "The Neurochemistry of Music." *Trends in Cognitive Sciences* 17, no. 4 (April 2013): 179–193. Doi: 10.1016/j.tics.2013.02.007

Chenausky, Karen, Andrea Norton, Helen Tager-Flusberg, and Gottfried Schlaug. "Auditory-Motor Mapping Training: Comparing the Effects of a Novel Speech Treatment to a Control

Treatment for Minimally Verbal Children with Autism." *PloS One* 11 (2016): e0164930. Doi: 10.1371/journal.pone.0164930.

Dolan, Eric. "Listening to the Music You Love Will Make Your Brain Release More Dopamine, Study Finds." PsyPost. February 2, 2019. https://www.psypost.org/2019/02/listening-to-the-music-you-love-will-make-your-brain-release-more-dopamine-study-finds-53059.

Emanuele, Enzo, Marianna Boso, Francesco Cassola, Davide Broglia, Ilaria Bonoldi, Lara Mancini, Mara Marini, and Pierluigi Politi. "Increased Dopamine DRD4 Receptor mRNA Expression in Lymphocytes of Musicians and Autistic Individuals: Bridging the Music-Autism Connection." *Activitas Nervosa Superior Rediviva* 51, no. 3–4 (2009): 142–145.

Ferreri, Laura, Ernest Mas-Herrero, Robert J. Zatorre, Pablo Ripollés, Alba Gomez-Andres, Helena Alicart, Guillem Olivé, Josep Marco-Pallarés, Rosa M. Antonijoan, Marta Valle, Jordi Riba, and Antoni Rodriguez-Fornells. "Dopamine Modulates the Reward Experiences Elicited by Music." *Proceedings of the National Academy of Sciences* 116, no. 9 (2019): 3793–3798. Doi: 10.1073/pnas.1811878116.

Gebauer, Line, Joshua Skewes, Gitte Westphael, Pamela Heaton, and Peter Vuust. "Intact Brain Processing of Musical Emotions in Autism Spectrum Disorder, but More Cognitive Load and Arousal in Happy vs. Sad Music." *Frontiers in Neuroscience* 8 (2014): 192. Doi: 10.3389/fnins.2014.00192.

Geretsegger, M., Cochavit Elefant, Karin A Mössler, and Christian Gold. "Music Therapy for People with Autism Spectrum Disorder." *Cochrane Database of Systematic Reviews* 17, no. 6 (2014). Doi: 10.1002/14651858.CD004381.pub3.

Gerry, David, Andrea Unrau, and Laurel J. Trainor. "Active Music Classes In Infancy Enhance Musical, Communicative and Social Development." *Developmental Science* 15 (2012): 398–407. Doi: 10.1111/j.1467-7687.2012.01142.x.

Hernandez-Ruiz, Eugenia. "Music Therapy and Early Start Denver Model to Teach Social Communication Strategies to Parents of Preschoolers with ASD: A Feasibility Study." *Music Therapy Perspectives* 36 (2018): 26–39. Doi: 10.1093/mtp/mix018.

Hyde, Krista L., Jason Lerch, Andrea Norton, Marie Forgeard, Ellen Winner, Alan C. Evans, and Gottfried Schlaug. "Musical Training Shapes Structural Brain Development." *The Journal of Neuroscience* 29 (2009): 3019–3025. Doi: 10.1523/JNEUROSCI.5118-08.2009.

Jäncke, Lutz. "The Relationship Between Music and Language." *Frontiers in Psychology* 3 (2012): 123. Doi:10.3389/fpsyg.2012.00123.

Janzen, Thenille, and Michael Thaut. "Rethinking the Role of Music in the Neurodevelopment of Autism Spectrum Disorder." *Music & Science* 1 (2018): 1–18. Doi: 10.1177/2059204318769639.

Juslin, Patrik N., and Daniel Västfjäll. "Emotional Responses to Music: The Need to Consider Underlying Mechanisms." *Behavioral and Brain Sciences* 31 (2008): 559–621. Doi: 10.1017/S0140525X08005293.

Kern, Petra, Mark Wolery, and David Aldridge. "Use of Songs to Promote Independence in Morning Greeting Routines For Young Children With Autism." *Journal of Autism and Developmental Disorders* 37 (2007): 1264–71. Doi: 10.1007/s10803-006-0272-1.

Kim, Cynthia. *Musings of an Aspie: One Woman's Thoughts about Life on the Spectrum.* https://musingsofanaspie.com/.

McKenna, Katie. "Sensory Processing: The Proprioceptive System." The Autism Helper. https://theautismhelper.com/sensory-processing-the-proprioceptive-system/.

Mendelson, Jenna, Yasmine White, Laura Hans, Richard Adebari, Lorrie Schmid , Jan Riggsbee , Ali Goldsmith, et al. "A Preliminary Investigation of a Specialized Music Therapy Model for Children with Disabilities Delivered in a Classroom Setting." *Autism Research and Treatment* (2016): 1–8. Doi: 10.1155/2016/1284790.

Morin, Amanda. "What is Early Intervention?" Understood. https://www.understood.org/en/learning-attention-issues/treatments-approaches/early-intervention/early-intervention-what-it-is-and-how-it-works.

NeuroScience News. "Autism and sensory processing: Avoiding the sensory overload at the root of meltdowns." July 5, 2019. https://neurosciencenews.com/sensory-overload-asd-14420/.

NurseJournal. "The Benefits of Music Therapy for Autistic Children." June 7, 2021. https://nursejournal.org/community/the-benefits-of-music-therapy-for-autistic-children/

Patel, Aniruddh D. "The OPERA Hypothesis: Assumptions and Clarifications." *Annals of the New York Academy of Sciences* 1252 (2012): 124–128. Doi: 10.1111/j.1749-6632.2011.06426.x.

Patel, Aniruddh. "Why Would Musical Training Benefit the Neural Encoding of Speech? The OPERA Hypothesis." *Frontiers in Psychology* 2 (2011): 142. Doi: 10.3389/fpsyg.2011.00142.

Schauder, Kimberly B., Lisa E. Mash, Lauren K. Bryant, and Carissa J. Cascio. "Interoceptive Ability and Body Awareness in Autism Spectrum Disorder." *Journal of Experimental Child Psychology* 131 (2015): 193–200. Doi: 10.1016/j.jecp.2014.11.002.

Schlaug, Gottfried. "Musicians and Music Making as a Model for the Study of Brain Plasticity." *Progress in Brain Research* 217 (2015): 37–55. Doi: :10.1016/bs.pbr.2014.11.020.

Schmid, Lorrie, Lauren DeMoss, Paige Scarbrough, Carol Ripple, Yasmine White, and Geraldine Dawson. "An Investigation of a Classroom-Based Specialized Music Therapy Model for Children with Autism Spectrum Disorder: Voices Together Using the VOICSS Method." *Focus on Autism and Other Developmental Disabilities* (2020): 1–10. Doi: 10.1177/1088357620902505.

Sharda, Megha, Carola Tuerk, Rakhee Chowdhury, Kevin Jamey, Nicolas Foster, Melanie Custo-Blanch, Melissa Tan, Aparna Nadig, and and Krista Hyde. "Music Improves Social Communication and Auditory–Motor Connectivity in Children with Autism." *Translational Psychiatry* 8 (2018): 1–13. Doi: 10.1038/s41398-018-0287-3.

Sharda, Megha, Rashi Midha, Supriya Malik, Shaneel Mukerji, and Nandini C. Singh. "Fronto-Temporal Connectivity is Preserved During Sung but Not Spoken Word Listening, Across the Autism Spectrum." *Autism Research* 8 (2014). Doi: 10.1002/aur.1437.

Srinivasan, Sudha M., and Anjana N. Bhat. "A Review of 'Music and Movement' Therapies for Children with Autism: Embodied Interventions for Multisystem Development." *Frontiers in Integrative Neuroscience* (2013): 1–15. Doi: 10.3389/fnint.2013.00022.

STAR Institute. "About SPD." STAR Institute for Sensory Processing. https://www.spdstar.org/basic/about-spd.

Valentine, Vikki, and Jon Hamilton. "Q&A: Temple Grandin on Autism & Language." NPR. July 9, 2006. https://www.npr.org/templates/story/story.php?storyId=5488844.

Zero to Three. "Parent Favorites." Zero to Three: Early Connections Last a Lifetime. https://www.zerotothree.org/resources/series/parent-favorites.

Songbooks and Products for Parents

Page 118 of the book talks about using a cabasa or sand blocks with your child. One place to get simple sand blocks, cabasas or other instruments is Music is Elementary https://musiciselementary.com/. "Sound Steps Set" and other sensory resources are available from FlagHouse Inc. https://www.flaghouse.com/Sensory-Solutions/Auditory/Musical-Instruments-Accessories-General-Sound/Sound-Steps-Set-of-6.axd.

Some other resources include:

Beat Bugs (children's animated TV series inspired by the music of The Beatles): http://beatbugs.com/.

Beaumont, Karen, and David Catrow. *I Ain't Gonna Paint No More!* New York Harcourt, 2005.

Boardmaker (visual supports): https://goboardmaker.com/pages/boardmaker-online-personal.

Boynton, Sandra. *Barnyard Dance!* New York: Workman Publishing Company, Inc., 1993.

Colandro, Lucille and Jared D. Lee. *There Was an Old Lady Who Swallowed a Fly*. New York, NY: Cartwheel Books, 2014.

Common Sense Media Lists. https://www.commonsensemedia.org/music-lists.

Dean, James, and Eric Litwin. *Pete the Cat: I Love My White Shoes*. New York: HarperCollins, 2010.

Dillon, Diane, and Leo Dillon. *Rap a Tap Tap: Here's Bojangles—Think of That!* New York: The Blue Sky Press, 2002.

Harter, Debbie. *The Animal Boogie*. Cambridge: Barefoot Books, 2011.

Lande, Aubrey, and Bob Wiz. *Songames for Sensory Integration*. All Music. 2009.

https://www.allmusic.com/album/songames-for-sensory-integration-mw0002279814.

The Learning Station. *These Are My Feelings*. YouTube. https://www.youtube.com/watch?v=ca8SUuG8vdA.

Martin, Bill Jr., and Eric Carle. *Brown Bear, Brown Bear, What Do You See?* New York, NY: Henry Holt and Co., 1996.

McDonald, Jill. *Over in the Meadow*. Cambridge: Barefoot Books, 2012.

Oxenbury, Helen, and Michael Rosen. *We're Going on a Bear Hunt*. London: Little Simon, 1997.

Paxton, Tom, and Karen Lee Schmidt. *Going to the Zoo*. New York: HarperCollins, 1996.

Paxton, Tom, and Steve Cox. *The Marvelous Toy*. Watertown: Charlesbridge, 2009.

Sensational Brain. "Free Resources." Sensational Brain: Creators of BrainWorks Products. https://sensationalbrain.com/free-resources/.

Shannon, David. *Duck on a Bike*. New York: The Blue Sky Press, 2002.

Websites

Autism Society. "Affiliate Network." Autism Society. https://www.autism-society.org/about-the-autism-society/affiliate-network/.

Autism Society. "The Autism Society's Online Resource Database." Autism Source. http://www.autismsource.org/.

Autism Research Institute. www.autism.com

Autism Self-Advocacy Network. www.autisticadvocacy.org

ESDM Training Program. "What Is the ESDM?" Early Start Denver Model. https://www.esdm.co/.

National Autism Association. www.nationalautismassociation.org

National PTA. "Start a Special Education PTA." National PTA: Every Child. One Voice. https://www.pta.org/home/About-National-Parent-Teacher-Association/Governance/Types-of-PTAs/Start-a-Special-Education-PTA.

Office of Comprehensive Transition and Post-Secondary Education—Beyond Academics Integrative Community Studies. "Beyond Academics." UNC Greensboro. https://beyondacademics.uncg.edu/about/.

U.S. Department of Education. "Transition and Postsecondary Programs for Students with Intellectual Disabilities." U.S. Department of Education. https://www2.ed.gov/programs/tpsid/index.html.

Voices Together: www.voicestogether.org

Facebook: Voices Together

Instagram: @voicestogethermusictherapy

YouTube: Voices Together Music Therapy

About the Authors

Yasmine White, MT-BC

Yasmine White has been a board-certified music therapist for nearly three decades working with children, teens and adults who are neurodivergent and/or have a neurodevelopmental condition. As the CEO and founder of Voices Together, she developed the VOICSS® (Vocal Interactive Communications and Social Strategies) model as a non-directive intervention. She is an author and co-author of peer-reviewed articles published in academic journals and white papers in national publications. She has enjoyed being a frequent guest on radio and television programs and presenter on her proprietary model at regional, national and international conferences.

She has two grown sons and currently lives in Chapel Hill, North Carolina with her husband Jim.

Voices Together and the VOICSS® Model

Many of the techniques, ideas and the general approach in this book are based on the VOICSS® model developed by Yasmine White beginning in 2007 within the non-profit organization Voices Together. The model has been deemed a best practice in the field by educators and administrators who have seen it in action and studied its impact on students. Having built Voices Together from a small nonprofit serving eight people to an organization serving thousands of people across North

Carolina, White is moving the organization forward to deliver a technology-enabled training platform for reaching anyone anywhere who may benefit from this model.

The VOICSS® model uses structured music-based interactions to prompt communication and social responses and connections. In each session, the VOICSS® model follows a pattern of brainstorming group responses, choosing a peer leader, singing reciprocal songs, listening and responding, and then reinforcing client responses. The non-directive approach, The 50/50 method is based on humanism. This process helps clients feel heard and validated, and helps them improve in goal areas such as self-awareness, self-direction, self-advocacy, social communication, listening skills, and, ultimately, independence.

The mission of Voices Together is to empower individuals who are neurodivergent and/or have a neurodevelopmental condition to transform their own lives.

Learn more at: www.voicestogether.org

Sonia Belasco

Sonia Belasco has spent much of her professional life working with young people as a mentor, tutor, and therapist. She holds an M.S.W. from Bryn Mawr Graduate School of Social Work and an M.F.A. in Writing from California College of the Arts, and loves fusing these two fields by generating accessible content themed around creativity, social-emotional learning, and therapy.

CPSIA information can be obtained
at www.ICGtesting.com
Printed in the USA
JSHW052014161121
20513JS00002B/3